D1201408

FROM
KAISER TO HITLER

FROM
KAISER TO HITLER
The Life
and Death of a Democracy, 1919-1933

BY BARBARA SAPINSLEY

GROSSET & DUNLAP
PUBLISHERS / NEW YORK

I wish to thank the following publishers for permission to quote from their books:

D. VAN NOSTRAND CO., *The Weimar Republic,* Louis L. Snyder, 1966.

F. A. HERBIG VERLAGSBUCHHANDLING, *The Two Germanys,* KURT VON STUTTERHEIM, English edition published by Sidgwick & Jackson Ltd., 1939.

HILL & WANG, Brecht on Theatre, Berthol Brecht, edited and translated by John Willett.

HOUGHTON, MIFFLIN CO., *Mein Kampf,* Adolf Hitler, 1943 ed.

INTERNATIONAL THEATRE INSTITUTE, *World Theatre,* Vol. 15, No. I, 1966.

SIMON & SCHUSTER, INC., *The Rise and Fall of the Third Reich,* WILLIAM L. SHIRER, 1959-1960.

UNIVERSITY OF NOTRE DAME PRESS, *Pan-Slavism,* Hans Kohn, 1953.

I also wish to thank Messrs. M. Frederic Simon of Granger & Co., Richard Hanser of NBC and Jeffrey Kay of Columbia College for their invaluable assistance.

B.S.
1968

To Greg and Ann

Contents

FROM
KAISER TO HITLER

Prologue

In August 1914 Europe went to war.

It was a war no one wanted and that no one seemed able to avoid. Its roots went back forty years.

In 1871 Prussia had defeated France in the Franco-Prussian war and taken from her two border provinces, Alsace and Lorraine. Bismarck, the Prussian Prime Minister, used to say, "A generation that has taken a beating is always followed by a generation that gives one." After 1871 Germany prepared for another war with France, and her Chief of Staff devoted ten years to working out a plan for the rapid capture of Paris when war came.

In 1890, when the German Kaiser allowed a friendship pact with Russia to lapse, the Russian Czar promptly signed a treaty, the *Entente Cordiale,* with France. Later, Britain joined them and the alliance of the three powers became known as the *Triple Entente.* Now Germany felt threatened. The Kaiser decided that he, too, should have a Navy as big as the British. The British were determined that their Navy be twice the size of anyone else's. The result was a fierce armaments race.

At the same time, Germany's ally, Austria, was having

1

The assassination of Archduke Ferdinand of Austria (pointing finger) led to the outbreak of World War One. Kaiser Wilhelm II of Germany (with cane) is at extreme left.

trouble with her Balkan minorities who wanted to leave the Austro-Hungarian Empire and join independent Serbia in a Greater Serbia. Russia gave these minorities her tacit approval; Serbia gave them outright assistance.

In July 1914, when a Serbian nationalist killed Archduke Francis Ferdinand, heir to the Austrian throne, the Austrians decided to punish Serbia and end the minorities problem for good. Russia promised all-out support for Serbia and called up her Army. Germany was already committed to help Austria in any Balkan dispute with Russia. Because France, her enemy since 1871, was allied to Russia, Germany felt she must act quickly and set in motion a plan for capturing Paris. The first step called for the invasion of neutral Belgium.

That, if nothing else, brought in the British, who had guaranteed Belgium's neutrality since 1839.

What had started out as a punitive measure by an aged and insecure Emperor against his small-Serbian neighbor became, without plan or design, a World War between major powers—the Allies (England, France, Russia, Italy and Japan) on one side, and the Central Powers (Germany, Austria and Turkey) on the other. Years later an exiled member of the Austrian House of Habsburg was quoted as saying, "We never intended *that*. What we had in mind was a *small* war."

In April 1917, when American joined in on the side of the Allies, the war was endowed with a purpose. America's intellectual and idealistic President, Thomas Woodrow Wilson, told Congress the war was being fought "to make the world safe for democracy." He also said it was "the war to end wars."

When the guns on the western front finally stopped firing in November 1918, the opposing armies faced each other at exactly the same spot where they had first met four years earlier. Eight and a half million men were dead; more than 21 million had been wounded; monarchies from the North Sea to the Aegean had fallen like rotten apples from a tree. And, as the next decade would show, the world was still not safe for democracy, and there was no end to wars or to militarism.

Out of the breakup of the Romanov, Habsburg, Ottoman and Hohenzollern Empires more than a dozen new democracies were established.

This is the story of the democracy that rose from the ashes of Germany's defeat. Its beginnings gave hope to all of Europe. Its fall, in 1933, had tragic consequences for the entire world.

PART I
The Bad Years (1918-1924)

1 Birth of the Republic

AT ELEVEN O'CLOCK ON THE morning of the eleventh day of the eleventh month of 1918 the guns on the western front were silenced. The Great War, as it is called in Europe, was over, and even in defeated Berlin there was dancing in the streets. Few in Germany gave a second thought to the fact that an Armistice is not a Peace. All they cared about was that the fighting was over and their sons and husbands could come home.

But home had changed. While the soldiers had been fighting and dying for Kaiser and Fatherland in the mud of France, their Kaiser had given up his throne and their Fatherland was on the verge of civil war.

The home front had been unable to stand the strain of war—though not one blade of German grass had been touched by the fighting. The people had been asked to make too many sacrifices for a goal that became more remote and less important. Casualty lists lengthened and Paris was as far away as ever.

Since March 1915 the British had been blockading Germany's seacoast, preventing much needed supplies from reaching German ports. By the final winter of the war, which

4

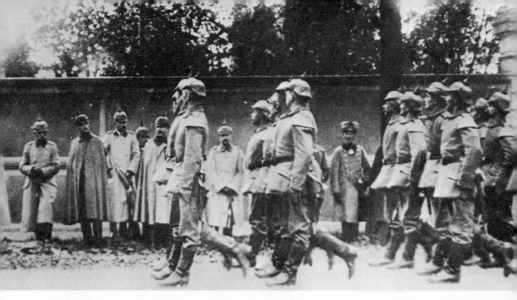

The Kaiser (far left) reviews German troops marching off to war.

became known as the "turnip winter," food and other commodities were so scarce that even coffee and cigarettes were being made from the hated turnip. Nearly a million old people and children died of starvation.

Regimes have actually been toppled by lack of bread. In 1792, demands for bread in Paris precipitated the overthrow of King Louis XVI and his Queen Marie Antoinette. In St. Petersburg (now Leningrad), women protesting the lack of bread in February 1917 set off the revolution that ended Romanov rule in Russia. In April 1917, inspired by the events in Russia the month before, workers in Berlin staged a one-day strike to protest a reduction in the bread ration.

From then on public disorder mounted. There were more strikes that had to be put down by ruthless martial law. There were more demands from the people and the politicians for peace along the lines suggested by President Wilson in his "14 Points" speech before the United States Congress in January 1918.

Since 1916 the Independent Socialists, formerly the left wing of the Social Democrats which had broken away in 1914 over financing the war, had been circulating their

5

Military leaders of Imperial Germany—Field Marshal Paul von Hindenburg and his second-in-command, General Erich Ludendorff.

clandestine anti-war "Letters of Spartacus." The German Parliament, the Reichstag, as early as July 1917 when victory still seemed possible, had passed a resolution calling for a "peace of understanding and reconciliation among nations without territorial changes or economic penalties."

Collapse and demoralization at home made it increasingly difficult to keep the troops in the trenches supplied. The troops themselves were less and less effective. The reservoir of young men had been used up. Replacements were now the too-young and the too-old.

When the Americans reached the front in the spring of 1918, and tipped the balance to the Allied side, General Erich Ludendorff, one of the Kaiser's two top military leaders, knew the German Army couldn't win. Until then the generals had reported only good news to the Kaiser. Ludendorff knew that the time for bad knews had come.

Although he was subordinate to Field Marshal Paul von Hindenburg, the Supreme Commander, Ludendorff was much the stronger personality of the two and had gradually assumed the decision-making role. Hindenburg, basically passive, merely approved Ludendorff's actions and took responsibility for them before the Kaiser.

A member of the Prussian land-owning aristocracy known as Junkers, Hindenburg was a professional military man. His family traced its soldiering back to the thirteenth century. He himself had fought in all of Germany's battles since 1866. In 1911 he retired because he could see "no prospect of war." But in 1914, at age sixty-seven, he was recalled when an unexpectedly rapid mobilization by Russia of her fighting forces caught the Germans by surprise. Hindenburg was put in charge of the 8th Army on the eastern front and won a smashing victory (which history now credits to Ludendorff) over the Czar's forces. As a result, he became a national hero.

In August 1916, Hindenburg was named Supreme Commander of the German Armies. He took with him his Chief of Staff (and some say, his "brains"), Erich Ludendorff.

Together, they became virtual rulers of Germany, even dictating to the Kaiser.

Ludendorff, too, was a Prussian and a professional soldier. But, a rarity in the Officer Corps, Ludendorff was not an aristocrat. He was known for his combat strategy of "defensive action," with which he achieved brilliant results on the battlefield. He also intervened in non-military matters when he felt that his actions would serve the cause of German victory. It was he, for instance, who made arrangements for the exiled Russian revolutionist, Vladimir Lenin, to be sent back to Russia after the Czar had been overthrown in February 1917. Ludendorff knew that Lenin would do his utmost to take Russia out of the war, thus freeing German troops in the east for duty on the hard-pressed western front. The canny Ludendorff was right. After leading his communist followers to power in the famous Bolshevik uprising of October 1917, Lenin signed a separate peace treaty with Germany and Ludendorff had his reinforcements. But even this could not save the Kaiser and his regime from final defeat.

On September 29, 1918, Ludendorff finally told the Kaiser that Germany must ask for an immediate armistice and must set up a new and more representative government that might be able to obtain favorable terms from the Allies.

That same day sailors on the ships at the German naval base at Kiel mutinied. They refused to carry out what they considered the suicidal plans for their Admiral, Reinhold Scheer, to challenge the vastly superior British Navy in a fight to the finish. Industrial workers in Kiel joined them in a general strike and by November 3 the rebel sailors' red flag flew victoriously from ships in the harbor. The rebellion spread along the coast to the northern ports. No one seemed able to stop it.

Shaken by the impact of the uprisings and the general unrest, the monarchy tottered. It was obvious, even to the autocratic Kaiser, that his throne was in grave danger. In a

Kaiser Wilhelm is briefed on the military situation by his two top commanders—Field Marshal von Hindenburg and General Ludendorff. Two months later—April 6, 1917—the United States entered the war.

last effort to hold on to his crown, Wilhelm II gave in to Ludendorff's request that he modify his royal powers.

Kaiser Wilhelm II, whom people all over the Allied world were now hanging in effigy, was fifty-nine. He had been Emperor for thirty years, inheriting the crown from his grandfather, Wilhelm I. Wilhelm II had been born with a withered left arm. Nevertheless, he was told constantly by his elders that he must grow up to be a warrior worthy of his grandfather. He tried to live up to this ideal and liked to appear in public in military attire. All his life he betrayed a weakness for martial display. One of his closets was filled with a variety of uniforms that he wore on different occasions.

Wilhelm II started his reign filled with energy and ideas,

9

many of them contradictory and few of them farsighted. In addition, he was willful and quick-tempered. But he didn't want to preside over the end of the Hohenzollern Empire. If changes were needed to preserve it, he would try to make them.

On September 30, 1918, the day after Ludendorff's ultimatum, the Kaiser announced that henceforth the government would be more representative. He appointed his cousin, Prince Max of Baden, as Chancellor of a cabinet that would for the first time in German history be answerable to the Reichstag. "Bad Max," as he was nicknamed by the public, seemed to represent the best of both worlds—democratic and royalist. As a Hohenzollern himself and heir to the throne of Baden, he had a stake in preserving the monarchy. He had had some political experience in the Baden parliament. He had a reputation as a democrat and was on record as favoring "peace with understanding" and a league of nations. Because he was a member of the royal family, monarchists and conservatives accepted him; because he was a democrat, liberals and socialists did, too. This very acceptability, in fact, posed a problem for the Social Democrats, the country's largest single party.

Since its birth in 1875, four years after the Empire was established, the Social Democrats had been dedicated to democracy, pacifism and the improvement of social and economic conditions. Their original hero was Karl Marx, though the party had long since lost its radical character. The question that now threatened to split it was: should it cooperate with the new government to stop the war (which fit its pacifist stand), or should it refuse because the new government was still a monarchy (which didn't fit its democratic stand)?

The party's leader, Friedrich Ebert, favored cooperation. His second-in-command, Philipp Scheidemann, did not.

This was not the first time Ebert had been involved in a party split. When he was first elected to the Reichstag in

1912, at the age of forty-one, the Social Democrats were fighting among themselves. One group, on the right, wanted to modify party goals to fit the changing times. Another, on the left, wanted to stick to the doctrines of Karl Marx. Two years later, in 1914, the left wing broke away altogether over the question of whether to vote the Kaiser the financing he needed for the war. Ebert, a tailor's son who had become a saddler by trade and an active trade unionist and socialist, now became leader of the Social Democrats who remained in the party.

Scheidemann also came from the laboring classes. His father had been an upholsterer and carpenter. Scheidemann's own career was different. He was first a printer, then a journalist, then the editor of a socialist newspaper. In 1903, at thirty-eight, he was elected to the Reichstag. In 1914, at the time of the split over war credits, Scheidemann had sided with Ebert. Now he disagreed with his party chief, but Ebert persuaded him to go along with Prince Max and they both were included in Prince Max's new cabinet.

Prince Max promptly cabled Wilson for an armistice. "The German Government requests the President of the United States to take steps for the restoration of peace . . . the German Government requests as a basis . . . the program laid down by the President of the United States in his message to Congress of January 8, 1918. . . . In order to avoid further bloodshed the German Government requests to bring about the immediate conclusion of a general armistice on land, on water, in the air. . . ."

But it wasn't enough. Wilson, the uncompromising and adamant idealist, was unwilling to deal with monarchists or militarists. To him they were "the constituted authorities of Empire who had so far conducted the war." The left-wing elements, too, were threatening revolution unless the Kaiser abdicated.

Meantime, Ludendorff had been having second thoughts. Although it had been his idea to ask for an armistice, he

11

abruptly changed his mind. Having, in effect, run the government during the war years, he thought he still could and wired all his commanders to fight on. This challenge to the country's leadership was too much for Prince Max. He promptly countermanded the order and Ludendorff felt obliged to resign. He was replaced by General Wilhelm Groener, former Quartermaster General, and, like Ludendorff, not a Junker. In fact, Groener was the son of a non-commissioned officer and had at first been passed over quite regularly for promotion because he wasn't an aristocrat.

Groener took on the responsibility of telling the German public that Germany had lost the war, thus letting Hindenburg, his commander, save face and stay a national hero. He also offered one solution to the problem of what to do with the Kaiser. He suggested that the Kaiser go to the front and get himself killed in battle. The Kaiser finally accepted the fact that he had to abdicate. Without him, it was still possible that the monarchy, in one form or another, might be saved.

On November 9, 1918, Wilhelm II gave up his throne and fled to Holland where he settled in the small northern fishing village of Doorn. He spent his remaining years writing memoirs that sought to explain and defend his actions as Kaiser. He also whiled away his time studying archeology, a subject that fascinated him. He died in May 1941, eleven months after Germany had conquered France in a new war and six months before the United States would again join in to turn the tide.

Prince Max, too, resigned on November 9, and turned the reins of government over to Ebert as head of the Social Democrats.

"I commend the German Reich to your care," he said.

"For that Reich," replied Ebert, "I have lost two sons."

The Social Democrats thus stepped into a vacuum and assumed responsibility on a caretaker basis. They also assumed the responsibility for signing the surrender and later the peace, and inevitably came to be blamed for Germany's defeat. The military and the industrialists got off unscathed.

It was Ebert's intention to call for a constituent assembly that would decide what form the new government should take. He himself preferred a constitutional monarchy aiong British lines, headed by one of the Kaiser's younger sons (the Crown Prince was as unpopular as his father), or a regent until a grandson came of age. Ebert disliked and distrusted social revolution, despite his party affiliation. "I hate it like sin," he had been quoted as saying. But in the chaotic situation then existing, debate and considered judgment were luxuries no moderate could afford.

Left-wing groups, which had used the new Soviet Embassy as headquarters and had been financed by the Russians until the Kaiser expelled the Soviet Ambassador, were

The ex-Kaiser in exile at Doorn, Holland. He died in May, 1941.

taking matters into their own hands. On November 7, the Independent Socialists had proclaimed a "people's government" in Bavaria. The Bavarian royal family, the Wittelsbachs, fled. Like falling dominoes, other German princes rushed to give up their thrones, some with dignity, others like characters in a comic opera. Revolution spread to. Germany's major cities. Berlin was paralyzed by a general strike.

Immediately after taking over on November 9, Ebert,

Rosa Luxemburg—also known as "Red Rosa"—the famous Polish-born socialist who was co-leader with Karl Liebknecht of the Spartacists, most radical of the leftist groups in postwar Germany.

Scheidemann and their colleagues sat down to a cold and meager lunch in one of the council chambers of the Reichstag, debating, as they ate, what steps to take next. Debate and discussion were something they excelled at. In Imperial Germany political parties had been little more than debating societies. A few blocks away, in the Kaiser's old palace, the Spartacists, a left-wing splinter group of the Independent Socialists led by Karl Liebknecht and Rosa Luxemburg, were preparing to proclaim a German soviet republic.

Both Spartacist leaders had just recently been released from jail. Rosa, a Polish-born revolutionary with a crooked back and a brilliant mind, had been a rebel all her life. A veteran of the 1905 revolution in Russia, she was known as "Red Rosa." She had been arrested in 1914 for "incitement of insubordination" and had spent the war years in protective custody. Her partner in revolution, Karl Liebknecht, was a lawyer by profession and a socialist by heritage as well as conviction. Wilhelm Liebknecht, his father, had been a founder of the Social Democratic movement and a friend of Karl Marx. Among his fellow socialists, the younger Liebknecht had a reputation for being a political maverick. He was also fiercely anti-militaristic and an ardent pacifist. In 1912, at the age of forty-one, Liebknecht had been elected to the Reichstag. He was one of a small group of Social Democrats who consistently refused to vote for the Kaiser's war plans. In 1916, though a soldier in uniform, Liebknecht led the first anti-war demonstration in Berlin. He was arrested and spent the next two years in prison at hard labor. Earlier in his career, Liebknecht had signed his political pamphlets with the pseudonym "Spartacus," after the slave who led a famous revolt in Rome in 73–71 B.C. And it was this name that had been adopted by the followers of Liebknecht and Luxemburg.

When the Social Democrats, lunching in the Reichstag, heard of the Spartacist plans for a soviet republic, Scheidemann was horrified and dashed to the window. He stuck

15

*A remarkable photograph of Phillip Scheidemann, the Social Demo-
cratic leader, addressing a mammoth crowd from the window of the
Berlin Chancelery in the tumultuous days following the end of the
war. Earlier, in a similar scene, he had proclaimed the new German
Republic.*

his head out and shouted to the gathering crowds: "Work-
men and soldiers . . . miracles have happened. . . . Everything
for the people! Everything by the people! . . . The old and
rotten—the monarchy—has broken down. Long live the
new! Long live the German Republic!"

For almost the first time in Social Democratic history the

16

party had met an emergency with fast action. Usually it had debated and discussed until the emergency was either past or past solving. Ebert was furious. "You had no right to proclaim the Republic," he said. "What becomes of Germany—whether she becomes a Republic or something else —must be decided by a constituent assembly."

But the deed could not be undone, and a Bolshevik take-over was, in any case, literally a fate worse than death to the Social Democrats. In order to rob the Spartacists of their most persuasive argument the Social Democrats had given the German people the Republic many thought they wanted. This Republic, so hastily proclaimed, was at least in moderate hands.

The crowds cheered. For better or for worse, without warning or preparation, and without majority approval, Germany had become a self-governing nation.

2 Legacy of the Past

NEWS ABOUT THE EARTH-SHAKING events at home reached the soldiers in the front lines slowly, sometimes as gossip or rumor, sometimes as verified report. But it always came as a shock. The average soldier in the line knew little about the war as a whole. He lived in a narrow world, bound in by the terrain he fought over and the comrades who fought and died at his side. He also lived in a world of illusion, fed by promises of ultimate victory by his leaders. The total pattern of the war escaped him—and the crumbling of German power, bled dry by enormous manpower losses and the crippling blockade, was invisible to the men in the trenches. Many among them were sick of war and wished its end; but there were those, too, who found the thought of defeat intolerable and viewed its arrival, when it finally came, as an act of betrayal by treasonous politicians.

One corporal, recovering in a military hospital from temporary blindness suffered in a British gas attack a month before, heard the news from a visiting pastor on Sunday, November 10. Twice wounded, twice decorated for bravery, but still considered a "loner" by his fellow soldiers, Corporal Adolf Hitler broke down and wept. Oddly enough,

The soldier with the long mustache (marked by X) is Adolf Hitler, future Nazi dictator. When this picture was taken during World War One, Hitler was serving in the Kaiser's army. He came home from the war bitter and disillusioned, convinced that Germany's defeat had been caused by traitors.

Hitler wasn't even a German by birth. Born in Austria, he nevertheless thought of himself as German, although he still was not a citizen of the country he so admired. Later, he wrote in his book, *Mein Kampf (My Struggle):* "So it had all been in vain. In vain all the sacrifices and privations . . . in vain the death of two million . . . did all this happen only so a gang of wretched criminals could lay hands on the Fatherland?" He could not bear the thought that Germany had met defeat on the battlefield. The only explanation he could accept was that the German Army had been stabbed in the back by traitors at home.

Hungry, demoralized, jobless and ready to tear down the old system, though not to build up the new one, the returning soldiers found themselves citizens of a democracy. Many of them, especially among the Officer Corps, frowned upon

19

November, 1918. War-weary troops of the defeated German army begin the long march home.

this new equality. They still believed, as the phrase from their national anthem expressed it, that they were "über alles," or better than everyone else. They also shared a common belief, which Hitler would soon make one of the underpinnings of his Nazi creed, that Germany, unbeaten in battle, had been subverted by cowardly and traitorous elements on the home front. Even so eminent a military man as Hindenburg would later express this idea in his memoirs. It was a sentiment that took hold among ex-soldiers almost from the first day of defeat and became part of the mood and the bitter philosophy they brought back with them to civilian life.

To make matters worse, the new Republic's delegates to the Armistice meeting had had to accept terms far harsher than they had expected. Some were impossible to meet. For instance, occupied territories were to be evacuated within fifteen days. But thousands of locomotives, railway cars and trucks had to be turned over to the Allies so there wouldn't

20

be enough transportation left to move the troops out of the occupied areas by the deadline. In addition, the right bank of the Rhine was to be demilitarized and sections of Germany to be occupied by Allied troops. All Allied prisoners would be released immediately but captured Germans would not. Worst of all, the British blockade would be continued. This calamity, which had reduced Germany to near starvation, was a major reason why she had sued for peace. And now this noose around her neck was not to be removed, as she had expected. It was a harrowing prospect.

Germany's delegates to the Armistice talks were given no choice. If they wanted an armistice, it was this or nothing.

It seemed to the troops straggling back from the front that while they had been away fighting, starving and suffering for the greater glory of Germany, those safe at home had robbed them of what they had been fighting for.

The Germany the Social Democrats inherited from the Hohenzollerns was a strange sort of nation. It was made up of a group of states that had not too long ago been independent of each other. These states had little in common, except for the language they spoke. Their gradual absorption in the nineteenth century, a few at a time, by the largest and most powerful of the Germanic states, Prussia, culminated in the Germany known to the modern world. The Hohenzollerns had been Kings of Prussia. Most Germans thought of themselves as citizens of their states—Bavarians, Saxons, Prussians, etc.—before they thought of themselves as Germans. In fact, Wilhelm II was less upset at having to abdicate as Kaiser of Germany than he was at giving up the throne of Prussia. This way of thinking—the tendency to identify with local instead of national interest—was called "particularism."

Even after 1871, when the Prussian Prime Minister, Prince Otto Eduard Leopold von Bismarck, unified the German states into an Empire, they still maintained their own dynasties and their own parliaments, which ruled over them independently of the federal government. Bismarck himself

21

continued to be Prime Minister of Prussia even after he became Chancellor of the German Empire.

Although the federal government resembled a constitutional government, in that the states were represented in the Upper House and the people were represented in the Lower House, it had no true federal power. The power was in the hands of the Chancellor, who was appointed by the Kaiser and was responsible only to him. The Reichstag, or Lower House, couldn't vote him out if the Kaiser wanted him to stay. If it voted against him, he simply dissolved it and called for new elections. Nor could it save his job if the Kaiser wanted him to go. It couldn't initiate any laws. All it could do was approve or disapprove of the measures

A famous painting by W. von Menzel depicts Wilhelm II, in 1871, being declared Emperor of Germany. Prussia's "Iron Chancellor," Bismarck, who made it all possible, is the booted figure in white uniform (center) clasping a helmet.

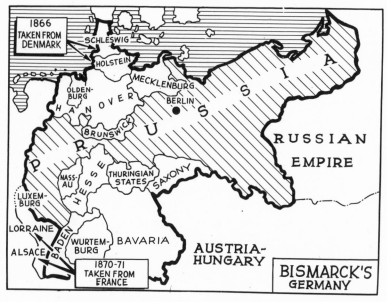

The Empire created by Bismarck, outlined in black, resulted from a series of annexations by Prussia, largest of the German states.

the Chancellor presented to it. The Upper House was equally ineffective, being virtually controlled by Prussia.

The Social Democrats knew about democracy only as a theory, even though they had been advocating it for years. They had never had a chance to test its practical application. They knew about the concepts of individual rights and responsibilities, cooperation and compromise from what they read in books, but they didn't know what democracy in action demands of leaders and citizens alike.

The German people, even those who thought a representative government would be an improvement over an absolute monarchy, were even less prepared for this exciting but perilous experiment. They had no democratic traditions to guide them. For at least four hundred years they had been taking orders.

Their churches, universities, philosophers and political leaders had been preaching the virtue of obedience and the vices of self-confidence and independent thought ever since Martin Luther broke with the Catholic Church in 1517 and initiated the Reformation.

Luther gave the people in the many separate German states their first awareness of a common nationality and a common tongue when, in 1521, he translated the Bible into German. He also encouraged the people to feel that as Germans they were different from non-Germans, and by stressing the old romantic Germanic folk tales and folk ways as a national heritage, he thus opened the door to a possible merger of the states into a nation. But almost immediately he slammed it shut and three and a half centuries would pass before unification took place. As a result of the Reformation, the Germans developed another division in addition to the political ones that already existed. They divided along religious lines into two groups, Protestants and Catholics.

Luther's appeal to the "German nation" to protest against the injustices of the Church, to seek "spiritual freedom" and "divine justice," was interpreted by the oppressed peasantry to mean that a protest against economic oppression would also be justified. In Bavaria, in 1525, they rose up in revolt against the Princes. Unorganized and disorderly, the revolt spread throughout southern Germany. Although at first he sympathized· with the peasants' plight, Luther hadn't really been thinking about political freedom when he talked about "spiritual freedom." He had no real confidence in the average man. In fact, his credo belittled "the people." He turned against the peasants, saying, "The brute populace must be governed by brute force." The Princes suppressed the revolt with brute force. Hundreds of thousands of peasants were killed. It was the last truly popular uprising in Germany until the people of Germany forced out the Kaiser in November 1918.

Luther preached that "the Princes of the world are Gods,

24

the common people are Satan. . . . I would rather suffer a prince doing wrong than a people doing right." This effectively denied the people's right to self-government or even self-defense against persecution. When he talked about "spiritual freedom" and "divine justice" he was referring to a man's private life. Publicly, the individual was under the absolute authority of the state and Luther believed the state could do no wrong. Therefore, whatever the state ordered a man to do, he could safely do without harm to his conscience. To Luther, the worst crime imaginable was "revolt against established authority" (except, of course, the authority claimed by the Pope of the Roman Catholic Church in the Vatican, against which he had revolted).

Luther denied that man had any control over his own destiny, in this world or the next: "For if as long as he has any persuasion that he can do even the least thing himself toward his own salvation, he retain a confidence in himself and do not utterly despair in himself, so long he is not humbled before God." Man's only hope for salvation, he stated, is in faith—blind, unquestioning, and above all, unthinking faith.

Thinking, said Luther, was evil. "There is on earth among all dangers," he wrote, "no more dangerous thing than a richly endowed and adroit reason, especially if she enters into spiritual matters which concern the soul and God." Reason therefore threatened faith and it should be blinded. He even offered his own interpretation of St. Paul to prove it. "Behold, this is what St. Paul in his epistles wants to show Christians: that these high and divine matters, which means both his divine being and also his will, his government and his work, are altogether above man's thoughts, understanding and wisdom . . . and must remain so."

In addition to hating reason and Catholicism, Luther hated Jews. He wanted the German states to get rid of them, and he advised that they be deprived of "all their cash and jewels, and silver and gold" and that "their synagogues and schools

Martin Luther, one of the great figures of the Protestant Reformation, left a legacy of anti-Semitism to the German people.

be set on fire, that their houses be broken up and destroyed . . . and they be put under a roof or stable like the gypsies . . . in misery and captivity as they incessantly lament and complain to God about us."

The southern Princes, against whom the peasants had revolted, never did subscribe to Luther's doctrines. They stayed within the Roman Catholic Church. The Princes of the northern states, more backward and poorer than those of the south, adopted Lutheranism wholeheartedly. This provided a fertile soil in which the authoritarian and militaristic Prussian philosophy could grow. It discouraged any kind of independent thought or action. It even discouraged the idea that the people were capable of making their own decisions.

In the three hundred years between Luther and Bismarck, the idea grew that the Germans were superior to other peoples and that through strength and discipline they could prove it.

Johann Gottlieb Fichte (1762–1814) was a professor at the University of Berlin at the time Napoleon defeated the German states at Jena in 1807. He advocated German nationalism, the superiority of Germans over Latins and Jews, both of whom he thought to be decadent, and a strong army to carry German ideals beyond her borders.

His successor at the University, Georg Wilhelm Friedrich Hegel (1770–1831), who was considered during his lifetime the dean of German philosophers, went a step further. He felt that history had followed a predestined course, reaching its peak in the Prussian state. Since men could only be truly free by moving with the currents of history, they should renounce their own opinions and submit to the Prussian state as the only logical choice. Democracy, he felt, was a menace to this freedom.

Hegel advocated war as a great purifier. It kept a nation ethically healthy, just as strong sea winds blow away the stagnant smell of a long calm.

Friedrich Wilhelm Nietzsche (1844–1900), whom the Nazis quoted regularly, tried to give his age new values because he thought that Christianity was bankrupt. He believed that only the strong should survive and that human sympathy only perpetuates the unfit and the mediocre. He did not believe in democracy because it gave an "illusion" of equality and denied the existence of a superman. Nietzsche approved of war and revolutions because times of strife bring forth great men. "Men shall be trained for war and women for the procreation of warriors," he wrote. "All else is folly." (Luther, before him, had had some thoughts on the role of women, too. "Let them bear children till they die of it; that is what they are for.")

Nietzsche was insane for the last eleven years of his life.

He continued to write throughout his illness and his later writings undoubtedly reflect his growing irrationality. Yet those who quoted him in support of their own prejudices took what they wanted from his writings, regardless of when he had writen them.

The German states were finally unified in 1871 by Bismarck, the son of a middle-class Berlin mother and a Junker father. He was a Junker by choice, not by upbringing. Like his mother, he was highly educated and sophisticated, something the Junkers, including his father, were not. Far from the civilizing influences of western urban society, the Junkers were crude in manners, uncultured, and often not too well educated, except in warfare. They were preoccupied with running their large estates in the eastern regions of Prussia. Though they were aristocrats they had nothing in common with the French and English aristocracies, which took a keen interest in education and culture.

Bismarck became Prime Minister of Prussia in 1862 during a parliamentary crisis over the military question. The Reichstag had already voted against increasing the size of the army and raising taxes to support larger forces, but Bismarck was determined to reverse this stand. Upon taking office, he stated flatly, "The great questions of the day will not be settled by resolutions and majority votes . . . but by blood and iron." He carried through the army reforms and collected the increased taxes even though they had not been voted.

In the next nine years he built the German Empire by fighting three wars in rapid succession. He defeated Denmark in 1864, taking over from Denmark the provinces of Schleswig and Holstein, which had some German-speaking inhabitants. In 1866 he defeated Austria and ended her dominant influence in Central Europe. At the same time he absorbed into Prussia those German states that had sided with Austria. In 1870–71 he defeated France and took over France's border

The philosopher who preached the coming of a Superman— Friedrich Nietzsche.

provinces, Alsace and Lorraine, whose populations also included some Germanic elements. At that point the remainder of the German states decided they had no choice but to join Bismarck's unified Germany.

What should have been the culmination of years of political action by the people was instead the result of the diplomatic and military maneuverings of a single man. From that moment, until the end of the Hohenzollern Empire in November 1918, there was no chance for the German people to take meaningful political action on their own behalf. Nationally, whatever needed to be done for them, Bismarck did. The best German brains withdrew from the national political scene, concentrating their energies on their local governments and on industry, both of which flourished.

Bismarck, as Imperial Chancellor, tried to appease conservatives and liberals alike while keeping Prussia in control of the government. He let military and social power remain in the hands of the Junkers, which satisfied the conservatives. To keep the liberals happy, he gave them nearly everything they wanted—free enterprise, modern administration,

29

secular education—so long as they didn't demand positions in government. His stand for secular education brought him into conflict with the Catholic Church, which didn't want to relinquish control of its schools. This struggle, called the *Kulturkampf*, resulted in the formation of a Catholic political party, the Centre. It had no real political philosophy of its own and sided with anyone who promised to protect what it considered the rights of the Church.

By 1880 Bismarck's struggle with the Church was called off, no decisive victory having been achieved by either side. His conflict with the Social Democrats now took on added force. To rob them of their campaign issues, he granted what their platform called for. He established compulsory insurance for workers against sickness, accident, incapacity and old age, the first such programs on the European continent.

"Give the workingman the right to employment as long as he has his health, assure him of care when he is sick and maintenance when he is old and the Socialists will sound their birdcall in vain," he said. Bismarckian Socialism, as it was called, didn't actually stop the growth of the Social Democratic party, but it did make the German worker value security more than freedom. It also gave him the feeling that he received his social security in return for political subservience, and that greater subservience might produce greater rewards. The idea that a government could be a servant of the people and that the rulers could be answerable to a parliament never even gained a foothold in Bismarckian Germany.

Germany's great poet, Johann Wolfgang von Goethe (1749–1832), was a symbol of German liberalism and the "good Germany," as opposed to Prussian militarism and virulent nationalism. He put his finger on the flaw in the Germans' self-image as it had been drawn and encouraged by their philosophers and statesmen: "I have often felt a sharp pang at the thought of the German people, so estima-

Johann Wolfgang von Goethe, Germany's greatest literary figure, was an ardent defender of freedom and liberal causes.

ble as individuals, so miserable in the whole. . . . Germany is nothing, but every single German is a great deal, and yet they fancy the very reverse to be true."

Bismarck had been eased out of government and politics in 1890 by Kaiser Wilhelm II, who wanted to run his own show. Eight years later, the man who had created an empire for the kings of Prussia was dead. But his memory and his legacy continued to influence German thought and action. Even in 1918, in the wake of defeat, many a conservative or monarchist still dreamed of a return to the glorious days of Bismarck and an expanding German Empire.

The new democratic government was thus born handicapped. The people had an inbred belief in the worthlessness of the individual and, except for the radical Left, they still wanted the sort of discipline, order and authority they had in earlier times, though none of these belong in a democratic system. The people also couldn't believe that their marvelous war machine had been defeated in the field, especially since none of the war's destructiveness had taken place on German

31

soil and no conquering armies were occuping their cities, except for a brief area along the Rhine.

Sick of warring, tired of sacrifices, hungry, craving peace and prosperity, many Germans gave lip-service to representative government. They even showed some enthusiasm for this "new start." But they were ill-prepared by education, training or tradition to do their part in making it work. Nor could they really accept the basic premise of democracy: that all men—no matter what their race or religion—are created equal.

3 Politics and Parties

THE ARMISTICE HAD BEEN SIGNED; the shooting had stopped. But the British naval blockade continued and Germany was hungry. Ebert's first statement as provisional Chancellor was a request that his countrymen stay calm and continue with their normal business.

"The political revolution should not interfere with the feeding of the population," he said. "It must remain the first duty of all, both in the city and on the farms, not to hinder but rather to further the production of food supplies and their transportation to the cities. The want of food supplies means plunder and looting and suffering for all."

One-third of Germany's children were already suffering from malnutrition and their death rate was three times what it had been before the war. The death rate of old people was also increasing at an alarming pace. The entire working population was seriously underweight and crimes increased, as Ebert had anticipated. The Americans, who began organizing relief operations for the starving people of Europe, including their former enemies, sent an expert to Germany in early 1919 to study the food situation. He reported that there was little meat, the bread was indigestible,

33

the beverages all *ersatz* (imitation), and that "from every point of view, the food is revolting." But neither he, nor anyone else, could persuade the British to lift the blockade. (Later the British would claim they wanted it as a lever to force the Germans to accept the Allies' peace terms.)

The provisional government, immediately upon taking over on November 9, 1918, tried to broaden its base. Ebert invited the Independent Socialists to join his cabinet. Although the Social Democrats represented the majority of German workingmen, the Independents spoke for the more radical and more militant sections of the working class. They were the people more apt to take to the streets with weapons to protest their grievances.

Hunger and insecurity stalked the cities of Germany in 1918. Many of its victims were children.

The split among the Independents, which would eventually result in their left wing breaking away to form Germany's Communist party, was beginning. The party, however, did stay together long enough to cooperate with Ebert, but only with certain provisos: the cabinet members must all be Socialists, political power was to be in the hands of the workers' councils (postwar organizations), and the constituent assembly must not be called until "the revolution was consolidated." They added that they would collaborate for only three days, just until the Armistice was signed. Ebert objected to the time limit and to putting all power in the hands of the workers' councils. This, he said, would mean class dictatorship. The Independents agreed to drop the time limit. Ebert felt it was more important at that moment to form a government than to argue over principles, so he accepted the rest of the stipulations, and three Independent Socialists joined three Social Democrats to form a cabinet. Liebknecht, still calling for a soviet government, refused to take part. Then the new government issued its second proclamation, a description of its aims.

These were not revolutionary, although the conservatives in Germany thought they were. The left wing of the Independents considered the statement a betrayal of "the proletariat." Its terms included all the standard socialistic and liberal ideas that the Social Democrats had been advocating for years. They reflected Ebert's belief in orderly peaceful progress through the ballot box rather than the violence and bloodshed the radicals preferred. Ebert already had enemies on the Left as well as the Right and both groups had access to arms. It was obvious that trouble lay ahead.

The day he took over the Chancellorship, and two days before the Independent Socialists joined his cabinet, Ebert, well aware of the troubles he might have with the Left, made a secret phone call to Army Headquarters. He asked General Groener whether he would support the new government in putting down anarchy and Bolshevism. If he would, Ebert

35

promised to maintain the Army in all its old tradition, power and privileges, instead of subordinating it to the civilian government.

This turned out to be a fateful step. With Army support, the new Republic did put down the the left-wing rioting that might have resulted in Bolshevik take-overs in various states. But it didn't prevent civil war from breaking out, and it did endanger democracy before democracy had a chance to grow roots. Ebert's deal with Groener insured the continuation of the military as the state-within-a-state that the November 1918 revolutionaries, and the Allied powers, thought they had destroyed. Germany was once again made safe for militarism. Most of the Officer Corps took an oath of allegiance to the Republic but never let up in their efforts to overthrow it. Groener, though, remained loyal. He resigned his command in 1920 and became Ebert's Minister of Communications.

In addition to the dangers from Left and Right, there was also an unrecognized danger from another group, originally designed as a bulwark against disorder, the "free-corps" (*Freikorps*). This was a volunteer policing organization, named after the famous volunteer corps that had been organized in 1813 to help liberate the Germans from Napoleon. As a result, it had a nice patriotic ring to it. But the 1919 Freikorps members were considerably less respectable than their Napoleonic forebears; they were mostly military adventurers, demobilized soldiers who had no jobs to return to, fanatical nationalists and unemployed youths. The Friekorps also attracted a number of officers of units that were, or were about to be, discontinued as a result of the limitations put on the size of the armed forces by the Versailles Treaty. It got its arms secretly from the regular army, the *Reichswehr*. The Freikorps was diligent in attacking liberal or left-wing gatherings, but much less so if the disturbance was caused by the right wing. Bullets were soon whistling through the streets of Berlin regularly; "unsolved" murders of left-wing,

36

liberal and even moderate politicians became commonplace.
After awhile these crimes didn't even make headlines and
the average citizen was no longer shocked or surprised by
them. The Freikorps also went to the aid of conservative
elements who fought republicanism in Poland, Finland and
the new Baltic republics.

In late November 1918, as the Independent Socialist
party was joining Ebert's cabinet, the Spartacist wing of that
party called for immediate sovietization of Germany and
world revolution. Early in December, some 3,000 sailors who
sympathized with the Spartacists barricaded themselves in
the former royal palace in Berlin and refused to leave. Ebert
had to call out the Reichswehr, which stormed the palace and
overpowered the sailors. This shooting down of republican
sailors by anti-republican soldiers angered many people in
Berlin. The Independent Socialist members of Ebert's cabi-

*Civil war in the streets of Berlin. Anti-communist forces, barricaded
behind piles of newspapers, are shown here in actual combat during
the Spartacist uprising of 1919.*

net resigned in protest. He replaced them with members of his own party. Now the cabinet was wholly Social Democrat and Ebert no longer had to adhere to the conditions the Independents had set. He could call for elections to a constituent assembly at any time.

On January 5, 1919, the Independents and the Spartacists, who were now openly calling themselves Communists, staged a "mighty demonstration" of protest in Berlin. The next day they demonstrated again. So did the Social Democrats. By January 11, 1919, the two groups were fighting in the streets. Ebert's Minister of War, Gustave Noske, a former butcher-turned-newspaper editor and trade-union leader, who had settled the naval mutiny at Kiel three months before, called out not only the Reichswehr but also the Freikorps. In four days of street fighting hundreds of radicals were killed. Some were officially executed; many were severely manhandled. By January 15, the Spartacists and their supporters were defeated. Their leaders, Karl Liebknecht and Rosa Luxemburg, were arrested.

While transporting them from military headquarters to the civilian prison on the other side of Berlin, the soldiers murdered Liebknecht; their excuse was that he had "attempted escape." They also beat up Rosa Luxemburg so badly that she died a few hours later. Both bodies were dumped into a canal. Liebknecht's was recovered and he was given a public funeral. It was several weeks before Rosa's body was found.

Now that peace of a sort was restored, the Social Democrats set up elections for the constituent assembly. On January 19 more than 30 million people went to the polls. Anyone over twenty could vote and, for the first time in German history, this included women. Voters chose a slate of representatives through an elaborate system of proportional representation that assured each of the country's many parties its fair share of delegates. The results were gratifying to the

38

middle-of-the-roaders, especially Ebert and the Social Democrats.

The Social Democrats won 163 seats. The Catholic Centre won 91. Together they controlled well over half of the Reichstag.

The remaining 167 seats were divided as follows:

75 seats were held by the Democratic Party, a liberal republican group formed in 1918 by the left wing of the National Liberal party, which under the Empire had represented industrial views. It was favored by liberal industrialists and financiers, professional people and educators.

44 seats went to the National People's party, an extreme right-wing group that had started out as the National Conservative party, spokesmen for the Prussian landowners when the Empire was founded in 1871. During the November 1918 revolution it had changed its name but not its political philosophy. Its leader, Alfred Hugenberg, a former director of the Krupp munitions works who now held controlling interests in newspapers and motion picture companies, had been co-founder in the 1880's of a patriotic organization called the All-German League. This organization advocated the creation of a state that would include all Nordic peoples, not only German-speaking, wherever they lived.

22 seats were won by the Independent Socialists.

19 seats went to the People's party, the right wing of the old National Liberal party, which stood for both the equality of citizens and the protection of private property, and wasn't yet sure whether it favored a monarchy or not.

The remaining seven seats were divided among the rest of the splinter and fringe groups.

It seemed that only a minority wanted either kings or commissars. The new assembly was predominantly middle-class, leaning ever so slightly to the left of center.

The assembly chose Weimar, in the state of Thuringia, as the meeting place of the constitutional convention for

Friedrich Ebert, a Social Democrat, was the first Chancellor and then the first President of the new Republic. Here, hat held high, he conducts a military inspection.

two reasons, one political and one psychological. Berlin was the center of radicalism and still showed the scars of the street-fighting of the month before. But, equally important, the new government wanted the Allies, as well as its own people, to know that Germany was returning to the humanist tradition of Goethe and not to the militaristic tradition of Bismarck and the Hohenzollerns. Goethe had spent the last quarter of his life at Weimar and his name was permanently associated with that city. The names of Hohenzollern and Bismarck, on the other hand, were linked to Berlin.

The first thing the new assembly had to do was elect a President. It chose Ebert by a wide margin. In his acceptance speech the new chief of state declared that he considered himself a representative of all Germany, not just the Social Democrats. He added that he wouldn't forget he was a son of the working classes, but he warned the Communists and the Independent Socialists that he would fight any attempts to take over the government by violence. However, Ebert's election did not sit well with certain right-wing elements. The Officers Corps, Junkers, and other aristocrats hated the idea of having a former saddle-maker as their President.

Ebert chose Philipp Scheidemann as Chancellor. Because no single party had an absolute majority, Scheidemann had to form a coalition cabinet. He chose a combination of Social Democrats, Catholic Centre representatives and Democrats, who were just a little to the right of the Centrists. Both extremes—Right and Left—denounced the cabinet on the floor of the assembly, but it won a vote of confidence anyhow.

The new cabinet then announced its program. Internationally, it wanted (and naïvely expected) peace along the lines of Wilson's 14 Points, which included freedom of the seas, no trade barriers, arms reduction, withdrawal of foreign troops, creation of an independent Poland, return of Alsace and Lorraine to France, and the establishment of a League of Nations to guarantee and protect the independence and territorial integrity of all countries.

Domestically, the program promised education for everyone, a democratic army, collective bargaining between management and labor, plus freedoms of speech, press, religion, learning and art. This program, the new government believed, would qualify it for membership in the world community of free and sovereign democratic nations.

The sessions of the constitutional assembly in Weimar took place in an atmosphere of calm. Everywhere else in the country there was turbulence. And nowhere was there more unrest than in Bavaria where a new "people's government" had taken office. Its premier was the local leader of the Independent Socialists, a journalist named Kurt Eisner who really wanted good government and not personal power. Eisner stood for election after two months in office to give the people the final say on his young government. His party lost and his foes demanded that he resign. At first he refused, but finally on February 21, 1919, he gave in. As he was about to announce his resignation he was shot and killed by a young aristocratic counterrevolutionary.

It was one of Germany's most senseless murders. Eisner was already defeated. His death deprived the German Left of one of its least extremist leaders and it also set off a wave of revolt throughout the state. Workers formed a revolutionary Central Council and on April 4 proclaimed a soviet republic. The newly elected Bavarian government fled. Then the revolutionaries, as so often happens, began to purge their opponents, setting off a bloody civil war in Bavaria, in which both sides committed atrocities.

Finally, with Berlin presumably quiet, Minister of War Noske's troops moved on to Munich in Bavaria. They liquidated the soviet government and its leaders; in the process, they also killed off many who had nothing to do with the Communists. By now the Bavarians had had enough of bloodshed and martial law. They tended to blame the radicals more than the reactionaries. By the spring of 1919, Munich had become the center of right-wing extremism. Leaders of the Freikorps in the city began to plot assassinations of prominent Republicans. Their habit of branding any Socialist or Liberal to the left of center with the label of Bolshevism spread throughout Germany and even infected Allied circles.

A Bavarian left-wing intellectual named Gustav Landauer had written not quite three months before in the journal, *Die Republik* ". . . A few determined individuals supported the revolution. . . . They wanted to be creative, not merely tolerate things as they were. . . . All others need a long and intensive education in truly democratic institutions. . . . Of the minority, many were lost to the revolution the day after it took place. Before the revolution they were soldiers plagued beyond endurance; in the revolution they were death-defying rebels; on the day of triumph they were soldiers who had won salvation; the next day they were fearful and anxious Burghers."

The famous quartet known as "The Big Four"—Lloyd George of England, Orlando of Italy, Clemenceau of France and Wilson of the United States, shown in that order. They were the men who wrote the peace at Versailles and shaped the destiny of postwar Europe.

In France, too, the Republic was having trouble. The Peace Conference at Versailles had opened in early April 1919. All the countries that had fought on the Allied side were represented, but it was President Wilson, British Prime Minister David Lloyd George, French Premier Georges Clemenceau and Italian Premier Vittorio Orlando who really made the decisions. The German government had given its delegation certain instructions as a basis for discussion. It thought the conference would be a meeting among co-equals, especially since it had done the Allies' bidding in deposing the Kaiser and his generals. It had forgotten how Germany-as-victor had treated the Russians-as-vanquished at Brest-Litovsk two years earlier. Ludendorff then had exacted one of the harshest peace treaties in history, under which the Russians lost 301,000 square miles of territory and 56 million people.

Almost immediately, the members of the German delegation discovered that no one would talk to them. If they wanted to voice an opinion, they had to submit it in writing to the Big Four (Wilson, Clemenceau, Lloyd George and Or-

43

lando), who might or might not read it. In fact, no member of the German delegation even met an Allied delegate face to face, except when the final terms were presented and signed. The peace treaty was simply handed to the Germans on a take-it-or-leave-it basis on May 7. They were told that war would be resumed if they didn't sign in five days.

The terms were a shock. Germany was to lose one-eighth of her land—to France, Belgium, Denmark, Japan, the new republics of Czechoslovakia and Poland, and the League of Nations, which would govern certain areas under a mandate. Some of this territory was, in effect, being returned to countries from which Bismarck had taken it. The German Army and Navy were to be drastically reduced in size. And the German General Staff as well as the system of drafting men into the Army were to be abolished. Manufacture of arms was restricted; fortifications along the Baltic and North Seas would be demolished; and the Rhineland (bordering on France) was to be occupied by Allied troops for some years to come. But worst of all, from the Germans' point of view, was Article 321, the famous "war guilt" clause, which declared that Germany and her allies were responsible for the war and all the damage it had caused. This clause was a justification for the Allies to claim reparations, which were to be paid in gold and in goods produced in German factories for the next thirty years.

In vain, the German delegates protested. Each protest merely stiffened the Allies' will to vengeance. Even President Wilson, whose 14 Points had long since been forgotten by everyone except the Germans, agreed to the harsh terms, on the condition that his beloved League of Nations be endorsed. The European nations endorsed it, but, in a final irony, Wilson's own Congress did not, and the United States never joined the League of Nations. It took a second world war to make Americans recognize the advantages of belonging to a world organization. In 1945, the United States was one of the chief founders of the United Nations.

44

The Germans managed to get an extension of the time limit for signing, but on June 16 the Allies gave them an ultimatum. The government at home agonized for four days. Scheidemann, the Chancellor, and his cabinet resigned in protest rather than sign the treaty. He was succeeded by Gustav Bauer, another Social Democrat who had been Minister of Labor. Racing the deadline, Bauer and his hastily formed cabinet decided that the document should be signed. Finally, on June 23, four hours before the ultimatum was to expire, the new Reichstag agreed to accept the treaty by a vote of 237 to 138, with five members not voting at all.

Five days later on June 28, 1919, the British finally lifted their blockade of Germany. The date was the fifth anniversary of the assassination of Archduke Francis Ferdinand of Austria at Sarajevo in Serbia, which had been the flash point for the First World War. The British declared that the purpose of the blockade had been fulfilled now that the Germans had accepted the Versailles Treaty.

Herbert Hoover, who then headed the relief program for Europe's starving people, wrote to Wilson that once the world had "recovered its moral equilibrium" he wondered

Irate Berliners, in June 1919, march to the Reichstag to protest the terms of the Versailles Treaty.

UNITED PRESS INTERNATIONAL

if it would consider a peace obtained by "such a device as the starving of women and children as being binding upon the German people."

Hoover was appalled at the hatred for Germany he had found among the English and French. The French insisted that all German assets should be held for reparations payments. None of them should be used to buy food. The English were equally firm until the General of the British Army of Occupation in the Rhineland observed the hunger at close range and agreed with Hoover that Germany should be allowed to import food from neutral nations and export a few commodities to pay for it.

Even in America, Hoover found pockets of intense hatred for the Germans, so much, in fact, that he felt he had to issue a statement justifying his humanitarian actions. To those who asked why he fed the Germans, he replied, "From the point of view of my western upbringing, I would say at once because we do not kick a man in the stomach after we have licked him."

Because Wilson and the Allies had refused to deal directly with the warmakers—the Kaiser and his generals—it was the new democratic government that had to accept the peace treaty, sign away German territory, German people, German pride and German prestige, and appear to agree that Germany was responsible for the war.

In September of that same year, 1919, Corporal Adolf Hitler was in Munich, to which he had returned after his discharge from an army hospital. The Army, which still had him on its payroll, put him to work as an "instruction officer" haranguing street crowds with the right-wing point of view. As a paid "informer," Hitler was also instructed to keep a sharp eye open for radical elements that might have been involved with the short-lived soviet experiment in Munich. One of the groups he was asked to investigate by his military bosses was a tiny organization named the German Workers' party. If the Army had any doubts about the

46

The National Socialist movement gave Hitler a cause and a party. This idealized painting shows him addressing a meeting in the early days.

political orientation of this party, Hitler soon put them at their ease. After attending one of its meetings, he came away impressed with its philosophy and with the future role it might play in German politics.

The German Workers' party had barely 100 members. It preached a combination of socialism and nationalism. It did not admit the war had been lost. It drew a spurious distinction between "Christian capital," which it called national and productive, and "Jewish capital," which it called international and non-productive. It scorned the middle classes because they didn't understand working-class problems. Its list of hates far exceeded its list of likes. It appealed to Hitler and he joined its governing board.

Hitler had picked up his political philosophy, such as it was, during his years of poverty in Vienna before the war. The son of an Austrian civil servant, he was unable to get into either the Academy of Art or Architecture in Vienna because he hadn't graduated from high school. He developed a hatred for "gentlemen with diplomas," as he called intellectuals. He eked out a bare living doing sketches for post-

47

cards and some interior decorating, but he spent most of his time in political arguments with other Viennese derelicts. Their favorite targets were "money-lending Jews" and trade unions.

In April 1920 Hitler changed the name of his new little party to the National Socialist German Workers' party, which was almost immediately abbreviated to Nazi, and he codified its principles. The Nazis wanted a union of all German-speaking people in a Greater Germany, repeal of the Versailles Treaty, return of the German colonies, citizenship restricted to persons with German blood (which did not include Jews), an end to immigration of Jews into Germany and deportation of all Jews who had come in since 1914.

No political movement can make much headway without a supporting newspaper. And early in 1921 the party acquired a weekly newspaper, *Der Voelkischer Beobachter.* Where they got the money to buy it, the Nazis never said, but there is evidence to indicate that it came from the secret funds of the Reichswehr itself. Later that same year, Hitler founded the Storm Troopers, an outgrowth of the battalions of husky young men who served as bodyguards for party leaders, maintained order, and ejected hecklers at mass rallies. Hitler now had a going political party. In the next couple of years it grew steadily.

Every new catastrophe, every new setback to the federal government in Berlin, every new economic blow to the white-collar classes drove more of the disillusioned toward the Nazis. Many of the disgruntled were there already.

In their eargerness to weaken the nationalist and militarist side of Germany, the Allies did not see that their best safeguard against a rebirth of the Prussian spirit was a strong Republic, and that to become strong the Republic needed the support and assistance of the Allies. By forcing strong punitive terms on the defeated nation, as if it were still the wartime Imperial government, the Allies gave propaganda weapons to both the extreme Right and the extreme Left with which they could attack the new and shaky Weimar Republic.

As a preview of what was to come, a nationalist newspaper printed the following paragraph, bordered in black, on its front page the day the Versailles Treaty was signed:

"Today in the Hall of Mirrors at Versailles a disgraceful treaty is being signed. Never forget it! On the spot where in the glorious year of 1871 the German Empire in all its glory began,* today German honor is dragged to the grave. . . . There will be vengeance for the shame of 1919."

*Bismarck had proclaimed the German Empire in that same Hall of Mirrors on January 18, 1871, shortly after Paris surrendered at the close of the Franco-Prussian War.

4 Poverty and Putsches

On paper the Weimar Constitution, which was finally approved on July 31, 1919, was one of the most perfect documents of its kind. It took the best features from the American *Bill of Rights,* the British *Bill of Rights* and the French *Declaration of the Rights of Man and the Citizen.* It declared that all Germans were equal before the law. It guaranteed freedom of speech and religion. It forbade censorship. A man's home was safe from intrusion. Citizens under arrest had to be told within twenty-four hours what they were charged with. Education was not only compulsory but an obligation of the state to its citizens.

The structure of the government was also modelled on the governments of France, England and the United States. There was an Upper House, the *Reichsrat,* representing the German states, but no one state would have more than 40 per cent of the seats. Prussia would no longer be in control as it had been under the Kaiser. The Lower House, the *Reichstag,* represented the people. Delegates were chosen every four years by secret ballot according to a complicated system of proportional representation. The President would be chosen by the people in a direct election for a seven-year term and could be re-elected. Although he was Chief Executive, all his orders had to be countersigned by the Chancellor, whom he appointed. The Chancellor, in concert with a cabinet that he chose, did the actual governing. The cabinet was responsible to the Reichstag. That is, the Reichstag could approve or disapprove of cabinet actions. A vote of disapproval automatically meant that the cabinet and the Chancellor must resign. Then the President either had to appoint a new Chancellor, with the Reichstag's approval, or he could dissolve the Reichstag and call for a new election.

But there was one aspect of the Weimar Constitution that differed sharply from those it had used as models—Article 48, sometimes called the "suicide clause." Article 48 provided that if any individual state did not live up to its constitutional obligations, the President could make it do so by use of armed force, and that if public order and security were threatened, he could take whatever measures he thought necessary to restore them, including martial law. He could also suspend temporarily, in whole or in part, a number of the personal freedoms guaranteed by the Constitution.

There was supposedly a built-in safeguard against abuses of Article 48, which proved, in the end, to be no safeguard at all. The President was to report to the Reichstag immediately if he used the Article and the Reichstag could rescind it—*if* it had a workable majority to do so.

The framers of the Constitution were understandably eager to have a weapon ready for instant use against right- or left-wing extremists. But what they did was to make available to the enemies of democratic government a legal weapon with which they could kill it.

The enemies of the Republic wasted no time. The radical Left had precipitated the first postwar disorders, the Spartacist revolt in January 1919 and the civil war in Bavaria that spring. By the time the Constitution was approved, the Left seemed to be subdued. Now the radical Right moved to the center of the stage with the Kapp *putsch* of March 1920.

51

The military chief of the Kapp Putsch, General von Lüttwitz, talks to his troops on March 13, 1920, the day after they marched on Berlin and took over the government.

Dr. Wolfgang Kapp had been a minor civil servant in East Prussia, a Junker stronghold. His father, a liberal, had emigrated to the United States after the unsuccessful revolt of 1848, and Wolfgang had been born there in 1868. But the Kapps went back to Germany when he was only two and he grew up a fanatical believer in the prowess and promise of a greater Germany that would include all the German-speaking peoples of Europe. During the war he was active in a group called the Fatherland party, which called for a peace *with* conquest and annexation. He even accused the Kaiser's wartime Chancellor of being in the pay of the British.

Backing up Kapp in the attempted revolt were several top military men, including General Ludendorff. Kapp's troops consisted of a naval brigade headed by Captain Hermann Ehrhardt (who was also a Freikorps leader), the same force that had helped Noske suppress the soviet republic in Bavaria the year before. The spark that set off Kapp's rebellion was the scheduled demobilization of Ehrhardt's brigade under the troop-limitation terms of the Versailles Treaty.

On March 12, 1920, the brigade (5,000 in all) marched

on Berlin. Minister of Defense Noske had only 2,000 men to oppose it. He called on the Army. The top military leaders, quick enough to suppress left-wing uprisings, refused to support the government in fighting off the right-wing rebels. "Reichswehr does not fire on Reichswehr," said General Hans von Seeckt, General Groener's successor as Commander-in-Chief.

The government leaders, unable to defend themselves, fled. But before leaving Berlin, Ebert called for a general strike. The next morning Ehrhardt's brigade made a triumphant entry through the Brandenburg Gate, occupied the government buildings and hoisted the old Imperial Flag. Kapp declared himself Chancellor.

His first proclamation, on March 13, promised something to everyone. " . . . The government will fulfill its obligations under the peace treaty, insofar as it does not violate the honor and the life of the German people. . . . The government stands for economic freedom. . . . The government will ruthlessly suppress strikes and sabotage. . . . The government regards it as its most holy duty to protect the war-wounded and widows of our fallen fighters. . . . Every person must do his duty! Today work is the most important duty for any person."

But successful as they had been in rebellion, the Kapp conspirators didn't know how to govern. They had no plans. They expected to be greeted with joy by the Berliners. Instead, they were greeted with a general strike. Without water, gas, electricity and transportation, Berlin was paralyzed. After five days, Kapp gave up and fled to Sweden. His active fellow-conspirators also escaped abroad. The Ehrhardt brigade, deserted by its leader, withdrew through jeering crowds, and the government returned, saved by the one segment of the population that was dependably republican, the working classes. But stability and what America's first postwar President, Warren Harding, called "normalcy" were still far away.

The next crisis was caused by money, not men.

During the war the government had started printing extra paper money to help pay off the rising war expenses. The German mark, in 1914, had been equal in value to the American quarter. Four of them equalled one dollar. With more money in circulation and fewer things to buy, prices began to creep up and the value of the mark on the international market began to slip. By the summer of 1921 it took 75 marks to equal one dollar. At that moment the Allies presented their first reparations bill, a whopping $33,000,000,000, which the hard-pressed Germans said they could not possibly pay.

The Germans had still been living in an idealistic dream despite the harshness of the peace terms. This reparations bill not only presented their economy, their industrial production and their treasury with an overwhelming burden; it also dealt a blow to their individual and governmental morale. What was the use of working toward national prosperity if the profits were all to go to the Allies in reparations payments?

Since money, in economics, means both cash and credit, loss of confidence in the country's future affected its credit and contributed to the instability of its cash. The mark then began to go downhill still faster and the government lost all incentive to try to stop the decline—which it could have done by balancing the budget, stopping bank loans and raising taxes. Without credit, reconstruction would have been slower and people would have had to live more austerely, but they would have escaped ruinous inflation. But the government, in despair over the reparations demands, saw inflation as one way of foiling the Allies in their attempts to collect.

By 1922 it took 400 marks to equal one dollar in purchasing power; by January 1923 it had reached 18,000 and by July of the same year it had climbed to 160,000. Four months later the worth of the mark had sunk to the unbelievable figure of 4,000,000,000 to the dollar and the bottom wasn't even in sight. German currency was literally worthless. One's paycheck, received on Monday, had halved in value by Friday.

Merchants were using the U.S. dollar as their measure of value and priced their goods accordingly. As a result, it could take a man's life savings—and often did—to buy a loaf of bread. Savings accounts, insurance policies, mortgages and pensions were worthless. Widows, civil servants, teachers, army officers and pensioners—all with fixed incomes—could no longer survive. They turned to anything for a little food, a little money. They sold their belongings, family heirlooms, even themselves. There seemed to be no point in holding on to what few belongings were left, since they would soon be worth nothing anyway. Their morals vanished along with their bank accounts, and those

The visible results of inflation in 1922. Here a worker shovels a stack of the cheap money—his weekly salary—into a cigar box.

55

whose bank accounts were big enough to withstand the loss were equally demoralized. Life in the cities became an orgy of nightclubbing, gambling, vice, crime and exhibitionism. The loss of faith in the Republic kept pace with the declining currency. Many began to heed the siren call of the extremists.

But not everyone suffered. The big industrialists were able to pay off their business debts with the now-worthless marks and wound up owning their plants free and clear. At 4,000,000,000 marks to the dollar, a man who used to have a bank account worth $500,000, now had an account in marks in the trillions. It wouldn't buy him any more than the original $500,000 did. But he could pay off a prewar debt of 4,000,000 marks ($1,000,000) and still have trillions left. The man he paid would be getting less than one dollar in purchasing power but account books don't record purchasing power. The Army's war debts were wiped out in the same way. So were the public debts of the various states.

The outlook on the foreign front was better. Germany's Foreign Minister, Walther Rathenau, was a dedicated public servant with the makings of a great statesman. He came from a wealthy Jewish family in Berlin. His father had been responsible for the rapid growth of the electrical industry under the Empire. By the time he was thirty-five, the younger Rathenau was already on the boards of 100 different corporations.

Rathenau had foreseen the damage a British blockade could do to the shipment of supplies of raw materials from abroad to Germany. And shortly before the war broke out he had organized a successful program to administer materials on hand. It called for a greater reliance on synthetics and ersatz products, which would relieve the strains and shortages imposed by a blockade. Rathenau's plan, strictly enforced, made it possible for Germany to keep going much longer than the. British had anticipated.

After the war Rathenau helped found the Democratic

56

party. He represented the government at conference after conference to work out ways for Germany to both meet her treaty obligations and restore her economy. For this apparent acceptance of the terms of Versailles (called "fulfillment"), he earned the hatred of the nationalists and other right-wing groups. They hated him almost as much for being Jewish. In January 1922, at the age of fifty-five, he became Foreign Minister and began trying to improve Germany's relations with her neighbors. He started with Russia, a neighbor with whom Bismarck had always maintained a close relationship.

The Germans and the Russians, despite their conflicting postwar political ideologies, had one thing in common: they both felt hemmed in by Allied hostility and ostracized from the rest of Europe. In April 1922, the major countries were meeting at Genoa, Italy, to settle some old questions about international debts (including those of Czarist Russia, which the Communists refused to recognize). The Russian and German delegations, both of which were being ignored, slipped away to the nearby resort town of Rapallo. There, to the Allies' indignation, they signed a treaty of friendship.

The terms were unimportant. What was important was the effect on the morale of both countries and the long-term military side effects. General von Seeckt now sent German officers to Russia to school Lenin's army in the arts of war. Contingents of German soldiers—in violation of the Versailles Treaty—also underwent secret training in the distant reaches of the Russian Steppes. Von Seeckt also encouraged German scientists and industrialists, to go to Russia to help her industrialize and to work in Russian factories on weapons-development, which the Versailles Treaty forbade them to do at home.

For all of this, Rathenau, who negotiated the Rapallo pact, should have been given hero status by the nationalists and the military. But their hatred of him was too strong. Shortly after the Rapallo meeting, he was murdered, according to plans made earlier by the Freikorps leaders in Munich. An eyewitness to the shooting reported that the assassins were "two men in long, brand-new leather coats and helmets," and one of them, the one who fired the fatal shot, had "a healthy, open face; what we would call 'an officer's face.' "

This assassination provoked a public outcry. The cabinet fell and Chancellor Josef Wirth, head of the republican wing of the Catholic Centre party, resigned. He was succeeded by a political independent, Wilhelm Cuno, who inherited both the inflation and the unrest.

A month after Cuno took office, the French took a step that brought German to the edge of collapse and almost caused another revolution.

Obsessed by a need for security after two invasions by Germany in two generations, and led by an unyielding and vindictive Premier, Raymond Poincaré, the French felt they must control German heavy industry. In December 1922, despite a German request for a moratorium on reparations payments till it got its economic house in order, the Allied Reparations Commission declared that Germany was in default on its payment "in kind"—in this case, timber and telephone poles. The French used this as an excuse to march into the Ruhr, the rich valley that produced four-fifths of Germany's coal and iron ore. The workers in the Ruhr declared a general strike. The federal government in Berlin gave them financial help and moral encouragement. With the help of the Reichswehr, sabotage and guerrilla warfare were instituted. The French countered with arrests, even executions, but for seven months not a wheel in the Ruhr valley turned. The German economy, what was left of it, slowly ground to a halt. The French finally began to realize that the cost of the occupation was greater than the benefits. Something had to break the impasse.

It took a new Chancellor with some bold, if unpopular, ideas to do it.

Cuno, who had lasted less than a year, was succeeded in August 1923 by Gustav Stresemann.

58

When the Germans could not meet their reparations payments, the French occupied the ore-rich Ruhr Valley.

Stresemann, the son of a wholesale beer merchant, had entered the Reichstag in 1907 at the age of twenty-nine. He was soon recognized as the leader of his party, the National Liberals. After the war he founded the People's party and became a supporter of the Republic, though he was a monarchist at heart.

Stresemann became Chancellor and Minister of Foreign Affairs during a period known as the "grand coalition"— all the middle-of-the-road parties from the left-of-center Social Democrats to the right-of-center People's party were represented in the government.

The first thing he did was to call off the passive resistance in the Ruhr. He recognized that nothing could be solved and no compromise made on reparations until Germany's economy was functioning again.

So, at long last, did the Allies. They set up a committee of experts, headed by American financier, Charles Dawes, to first make a study of German finances and then overhaul them.

When Stresemann announced both the end of passive resistance in the Ruhr and the resumption of reparations payments, both the Right and Left exploded in protest. Stresemann had anticipated trouble. He had President Ebert declare a state of emergency under Article 48. This meant that Minister of Defense Otto Gessler and Reichswehr Com-

59

Gustav Stresemann —politician of the middle—who sought to steer Germany along a path of moderation. This picture shows him just before he became Chancellor in August 1923.

mander Seeckt were, in effect, running the country.

Bavaria promptly declared its own state of emergency and installed its own Commissioner with dictatorial powers. Seeckt, worried about the loyalties of the Army units in the Munich area, decided that the Army's future and his own as its head were best served by standing by the federal government. He warned the Bavarians that rebellion would not be tolerated. But there was at least one Bavarian group that didn't listen.

On the night of November 8, 1923, the new Bavarian Commissioner was speaking to about 30,000 people in one of Munich's larger beer halls. Hitler's Storm Troopers surrounded the hall and the Nazi leader himself rushed in brandishing a revolver. He shot at the ceiling and shouted: "The National Revolution has begun. This building is occupied by 600 heavily armed men, No one may leave . . . ." Then, resorting to his first use of the "big lie" technique (if it's outrageous enough and repeated often enough, people will believe it), he declared that the Bavarian government and the federal government in Berlin had been overthrown. A provisional national government, he added, had been formed and the Army and police were now marching on Munich under the Nazi banner, the Swastika, with a march on Berlin to follow.

Hitler herded the city fathers into an adjoining room and promised them that if they went along with his putsch they would all have key jobs in the new government he and General Ludendorff were forming. This would have been news to Ludendorff. He didn't even know of the putsch yet, and he certainly wasn't one of Hitler's colleagues.

The Bavarian leaders didn't react the way Hitler expected them to. They sat there and raised objections. Meanwhile, a Hitler deputy had gone to bring Ludendorff to the beer

A contingent of Hitler's Storm Troops that took part in the 1923 Beer Hall Putsch.

hall. Ludendorff was furious when he found that a putsch had been started without consulting him, but he decided to go along with it in the interests of anti-republicanism. While Hitler was busy talking to the General and attending to other details of his plan, the Commissioner of Bavaria and his colleagues managed to get away.

Hitler had another unpleasant surprise in store. The Reichswehr, which he had assumed would follow him, was following Seeckt instead and the police were following the Army. Hitler knew that his troops, adequate though they were for terrorism and breaking up opponents' meetings, were not sufficient to challenge the Reichswehr and the police. He was ready to quit. But Ludendorff, now that he had thrown in his lot with the revolution, wasn't. He suggested that he and Hitler lead the Storm Troopers to the center of Munich the next morning and take over the city. He was sure that none of the soldiers would fire on him, their former commander, and also that they would join him and follow him to Berlin.

So the next morning, November 9, 1923, Hitler and Ludendorff, accompanied by other Nazi leaders and a column of 3,000 Storm Troopers set out for the center of Munich. They almost got there unopposed. But in the narrow street

Munich on November 9, 1923, scene of the attempted Nazi uprising, after order had been restored. The abortive revolt ended in a fiasco and Hitler was arrested.

leading to the War Ministry, a column of police barred the way. Ludendorff's name had no magic for them; they were not the Army. No one knows who fired the first shot, but a shot was fired and a barrage followed. Hitler fled. Other Nazis fell to the ground. Only Ludendorff continued to march forward but no one followed him. The putsch was over.

Ludendorff was arrested on the spot, Hitler two days later, on November 11, 1923, the fifth anniversary of the Armistice. Both, plus a number of lesser Nazis, were tried for treason. The trial lasted for twenty-four days and made the front pages of every newspaper in Germany.

Hitler used the courtroom as a public platform from which to speak to all of Germany. It was the first time he had had an audience outside of Bavaria. He cried out that the signers of the Armistice ("the November criminals," he called them) and of the Versailles Treaty were the real traitors.

"I have hopes that the old cockade will be lifted from the dirt, that the old colors will be unfurled to flutter again, that expiation will come before the tribunal of God," he cried. ". . .*That* court will judge us, the Quartermaster General of the old Army, its officers and soldiers, who as Germans wanted only the best for their people and Fatherland. . . ."

Ludendorff was acquitted. The next year, 1924, he was elected to the Reichstag as a Nazi deputy. Then he founded his own minority right-wing party and in 1925 ran on its ticket for President. He polled only one per cent of the vote. That was, in effect, Ludendorff's last public effort and he retired from politics.

Hitler and his aides went to jail. Hitler was sentenced to five years but he served only nine months. During that brief period he began work on his book, *Mein Kampf,* in which he blueprinted quite accurately just what he planned to do to gain power and what he planned to do with it once he had it. Hitler had learned in the putsch that a frontal attack on the established government by a rebel minority doesn't work, that to achieve power he would have to operate within the framework of the law, even though he planned to subvert it at the first opportunity. For that he needed money, and for money he needed the support of the very rich. He had also learned that he *must* have the Army with him.

His book became a best-seller in Germany, and from 1925 on Hitler made enough in royalties from it to live quite comfortably. The rest of the world ignored it. The rest of the world thought the funny little man with the Charlie Chaplin mustache, who had run away at the sound of the first shot, was finished.

For a while it seemed that the rest of the world was right. With Stresemann taking decisive and fast action on the questions of inflation, left-wing agitation, and the various other problems that had plagued the country since 1918, it looked as if Germany had passed its fiscal and political crises and was beginning to achieve relative stability. The bad years appeared to be over.

5 The Arts:
"A Wonderful Ferment..."

THE SOCIAL AND POLITICAL UPHEAVAL THAT threatened Germany's economy and infant democracy during the bad years of the 1920's had the exact opposite effect on her culture. The arts had never been more flourishing, more exciting or more inventive since the golden age of German culture in the eighteenth century—the years when Goethe was writing dramas and Beethoven composing symphonies.

Germany was then a collection of small states loosely linked through a common language. After Bismarck unified those states into a German Empire with a centralized government in 1871, culture took a back seat to Prussian imperialism and militarism. Apparently, cultural growth and centralized government could not co-exist in a Prussianized Germany.

The Prussian tended to be anti-intellectual. He echoed Luther in his distrust of reason and independent thought. Otto Zarek, a Jewish writer and theatrical producer, wrote of the German intellectual, "Every independent mind is a stranger in his own country." Heinrich Mann, not Prussian either, blamed the intellectuals themselves for this. Mann wanted them to build a society based on reason and justice and criticized them for doing nothing to lessen the distance between themselves and the rest of the people. He didn't seem to think the Prussian influence was sufficient excuse for the alienation of the intellectual.

In Imperial Germany, creative people had preferred to live as far as possible from the seat of power, which was Berlin, capital of both Prussia and the Empire. Provincial theatre and regional schools of writing were then the custom. After the war, creative people flocked to Berlin. The capital city suddenly became the center of political radicalism and artistic experimentation. The military defeat in November 1918 had been a defeat for Prussian ideology as well, and the non-Prussian was suddenly freed of his intellectual chains. Most of those who made Berlin the artistic center of Europe in the 1920's came from states other than Prussia and many came from states that had joined the Empire reluctantly in the first place.

Not only Germans were drawn to Berlin. The new and heady freedom that transformed it into a city of midnight lights, glitter and bold new ideas drew people from the rest of Europe, too. Berlin began to rival Paris as the most exciting city in Europe.

William L. Shirer, newspaperman and author of *Berlin Diary* and *The Rise and Fall of the Third Reich,* first came to Berlin in the 1920's as a young reporter who had already worked in London and Paris. He wrote: "A wonderful ferment was working in Germany. Life seemed more free, more modern, more exciting than in any place I had ever seen. Nowhere else did the arts or the intellectual life seem so lively. In contemporary writing, painting and architecture, in music and drama, there were new currents and fine talents. And everywhere there was an accent on youth. . . . People were filled with an enormous zest for living to the full and in complete freedom. The old oppressive Prussian spirit seemed to be dead and buried."

Toward the end of the twenties, the young English writer,

There was another side to the mood of the twenties—a zest for freedom and the good life. German night clubs were noted for their air of carefree gaiety.

Christopher Isherwood, came to Berlin and earned his room and board by tutoring English. By then, Shirer's "wonderful ferment" had given way to a carnival atmosphere of feverish activity designed to cover up the loss of faith in freedom.

Isherwood's *Berlin Stories* showed, through his characters—his landlady, other boarders, his pupils—the dreadful after-effects of the economic inflation, the loss of moral standards, the growing distrust of democracy and the growth of Nazism and anti-Semitism.

But even as the Republic, unwittingly, moved toward its final years, the Germans made some of their greatest contributions to art and cultural life. They showed the rest of the world exciting new ways to make movies that revolutionized

67

film techniques. Their innovations in drama and dramatic production stimulated theatrical efforts throughout Europe and America. In the field of the novel, they produced many outstanding works, including one of the authentic masterpieces of the twentieth century. And they also—if that weren't enough—introduced a new school of architecture that influenced builders everywhere.

Germans were the first to use the motion picture camera as if it were the human eye instead of having it fixed in one place. They were the first to move out of the studios and film movies on actual locations. They introduced the use of symbols to set moods and draw characters. In the theatre, Max Reinhardt introduced the revolving stage and Erwin Piscator, the stage treadmill, both of which produced a greater sense of movement and reality. Walter Gropius, through the Bauhaus, fathered industrial design, the graphic arts and set architecture off in bold, new directions.

The "wonderful ferment" didn't ignore the harsh realities. Writers, artists, film-makers and playwrights used the life around them as raw material. They were among the first to see and the first to describe the people's disillusion with democracy and their drift to the extremes of Right and Left.

During the first few postwar years, the arts were primarily escapist. Max Reinhardt staged costume and historical spectacles. Carl Zuckmayer based his plays on German folklore. (Yet it was *The Captain from Kopenick,* a satire on the German's blind obedience to a uniform regardless of who wears it, that turned out to be his best-known play.)

The first postwar movies were based on folklore and ancient German myths. Then the movie-makers turned to horror films, which were also a form of escape from the disasters of civil war and inflation. The most famous of these was *The Cabinet of Dr. Caligari,* a story told by a madman, although the audience does not know until the last scene that he is mad.

Among writers during this period, Franz Werfel wrote primarily historical novels. His best-known works, *The Forty Days of Musa Dagh* and *The Song of Bernadette,* were written later. Stefan Zweig and Emil Ludwig wrote biographies of people who were already famous. Sigmund Freud and Mary Baker Eddy were among the subjects of Zweig's biographies, while Ludwig wrote of such people as Goethe, Rembrandt and Napoleon. (In fact, Ludwig turned out so many biographies so rapidly that his critics accused him of manufacturing biographies "on a conveyor belt.")

In a few years the escapist mood passed and the artists and writers began to tackle contemporary subjects. Movie-makers produced "street films," so called because they were literally about life in the streets and were actually filmed in the streets instead of on studio sets. They had such titles as *The Street, The Joyless Street* (in which Greta Garbo

Director and producer Max Reinhardt, whose theater in Berlin became famous for the spectacles he staged.

THE MUSEUM OF MODERN ART/FILM STILLS ARCHIVE

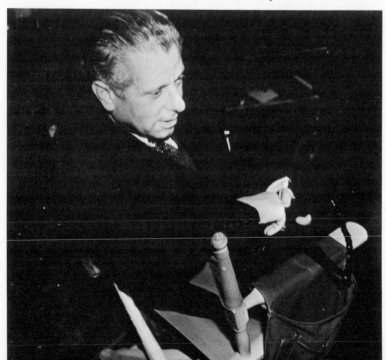

Scenes from four famous German movies of the twenties

(Upper left) The Threepenny Opera, based on the play by Bertolt Brecht; (Upper right) Metropolis, *a film that influenced Hitler; (Lower left)* The Blue Angel, *with Marlene Dietrich and Emil Jannings (center); (Lower right)* M, *the Fritz Lang production that made Peter Lorre a star.*

70

made her film debut), and *Tragedy of the Streets.* They showed the problems of the average man during the early chaotic years of the Weimar Republic. Then movies attacked militarism [Fritz Lang's *Mädchen in Uniform* ("Girl in Uniform")], and mechanization (Lang's *Metropolis*).

Hitler saw *Metropolis* and was enormously impressed by it. He recognized that he could turn its message upside down and make it an argument for fascism. Immediately after he became Chancellor, he had his propaganda minister, Paul Josef Goebbels, send for Lang to ask him to make Nazi propaganda films. Lang said he'd be delighted, left Goebbels' office, and went directly to his bank where he drew out all his money. Then he raced home to pack a bag, and caught the first train out of Germany.

Other famous films of the twenties were Josef von Sternberg's *The Blue Angel,* which launched Marlene Dietrich, and Lang's *M*, the story of a child murderer, which made Peter Lorre a star. *M* was the last great German film. The German film industry went into an eclipse during the Nazi regime. It has not yet recovered.

For the theatre, Bertolt Brecht, who sided with the Left and later joined the Communist party, wrote plays that challenged capitalism, city life (which he called a jungle), social hypocrisies, war and fascism. His most famous work during the twenties was *Three Penny Opera.* Kurt Weill, an innovator in music, wrote the score, and Weill's wife, Lotte Lenya, starred. *Three Penny Opera* was based on *The Beggar's Opera,* written in 1727 by the Englishman, John Gay. It burlesqued modern society by showing it as an empire ruled by a criminal underworld.

Erwin Piscator, a left-wing director, introduced the concept of "total theatre," in which settings, costumes, lighting, performance and subject matter were one integrated whole.

Playwright and poet Ernst Toller wrote about politics and also engaged in political action. A friend of Kurt Eisner, he served as a member of Eisner's short-lived "people's government" in Bavaria in 1919. Afterwards, he had second thoughts about the regime and tried to persuade the Bavarian leftists to act more moderately. When these efforts at persuasion failed, he began to preach moderation in his plays.

Writers of fiction also became more topical. Thomas Mann, brother of Heinrich and one of the great novelists of this century, had been an ardent supporter of the Kaiser and the war. After the Armistice, he turned away from militarism and became an equally ardent supporter of the Republic and democracy. In fact, he decided that democracy was man's only hope. In his greatest book, *The Magic Mountain*, which appeared in 1924, he seemed to doom modern bourgeois, middle-class civilization. Yet at the end, Mann had his hero leave the Magic Mountain and return to the hardships of real life, a sign of hope in his bleak picture of the world.

Franz Kafka wrote mostly about man's attempt to determine what in life is real and what is illusory. Baffled by experience, paralyzed by indecision, his heroes usually ended up totally frustrated. His most famous novels, *The Trial* and *The Castle,* were published after his death in 1924.

Erich Maria Remarque's *All Quiet on the Western Front,* published in 1929, was the first of his many anti-war novels. He followed it with *The Road Back,* a story concerning the problems of soldiers returning from war, and later with *Three Comrades,* about three veterans during the depression. Still later, in exile from Hitler's Germany, he wrote *Flotsam and Jetsam* and *Arch of Triumph,* both about refugees.

Arnold Zweig, one of the few Prussians on the literary scene, wrote a cycle of four anti-war novels. The third and most famous was *The Case of Sérgeant Grischa,* the story of a simple-minded Russian prisoner of war hopelessly caught in the clutches of military law.

After the anti-war books came novels that drew unforgettable portraits of life in the bleak and feverish twenties.

72

Germany's greatest writer of modern times, Thomas Mann, struck a note of pessimism and impending doom in his novel, The Magic Mountain.

Chief among them were Hans Fallada's *Little Man, What Now?,* an account of a young family crushed by economic disaster, and Lion Feuchtwanger's *Success,* debunking the postwar prosperity of the few during the inflation.

The artists, too, showed life as it really was. Käthe Kollwitz did charcoal portraits revealing the actual, individual miseries of the poor. George Grosz produced biting satirical drawings of manners, customs and hypocrisies of the frenzied party-going Berlin life. The people looked at them, admired them, and seldom realized that their own way of life was being criticized.

Beside the boom in the arts there was still another reason for Berlin's reputation as a cultural center. This was the presence of the brilliant scientist, Albert Einstein. A cult grew up around him and his new theory of relativity, and it became a status symbol to be able to say you knew him personally. But, unfortunately, few of his admirers understood what he was talking about.

They made a fad of the word "relativity" and used it to excuse inconsistency and vacillation. Since everything was "relative," they said, only "a man of yesterday" who was "untouched by the spirit of relativity" would stick to an opinion or taste. Berlin in the 1920's worshipped at Einstein's feet. Germany in the 1930's drove him out because he was Jewish.

The innovations in art, architecture and design developed by the Bauhaus group during this period were fully as exciting as the achievements in the other arts.

The Bauhaus (which means "a house for building") was founded in 1919 by Walter Gropius. He was a young Berlin architect who had already made a name for himself by designing simple, functional buildings with no adornment, something Germany had never seen before.

In 1915, the Grand Duke of Weimar offered Gropius the directorship of his Grand Ducal School of Arts and Crafts. (This was the same Duchy where Goethe had spent the last twenty-five years of his life, by invitation of an earlier Grand Duke of Weimar.) By the time Gropius took the job, the Duchy had become a republic with a socialist government and the constitutional convention was meeting there.

Gropius announced a new school or training laboratory for art, architecture and design. Anything from coffee cups to a model for an entire city could be designed and built there. The guiding principle was to be function—the use for which the object was intended would be the only consideration in its design. From the Bauhaus came the important new professions of industrial design and graphic arts. Among the teachers were the American-born artist Lyonel Feininger, the Swiss Paul Klee and the Russian abstract painter, Wasiliy Kandinsky.

74

People came to the Bauhaus from all over Germany—returning soldiers with artistic ambitions, students from art schools, apprentice craftsmen. Two out of every three who turned up in Weimar had to be turned down for lack of space. There was no tuition fee, and for those who couldn't even afford room rent Gropius persuaded the Weimar authorities to provide a free dormitory.

Almost from the first, there was conservative opposition to the Bauhaus. Local right-wing groups thought Gropius'

The genius whose theory of relativity changed our picture of the universe—Albert Einstein. Later, he had to flee Hitler's Germany because he was a Jew.

Walter Gropius founded a revolutionary school of architecture—the Bauhaus.

ideas were radical and probably dangerous. The opposition grew as the right-wing parties grew. In 1924, the local government, now in right-wing hands, cut the school's budget by two-thirds. Gropius then decided to move it elsewhere, where the atmosphere would be more sympathetic.

He chose Dessau, a small industrial city in what is now East Germany. Dessau had a farsighted, imaginative mayor who saw to it that the Bauhaus got enough money to have its own workshops, stage, lecture halls and living quarters. Gropius himself designed the buildings and Marcel Breuer, a former student who joined the faculty, designed the furnishings.

Even though Dessau was more liberal than Weimar, the unconventional artists with their unusual dress and odd ideas began to stir up opposition there, too. More and more Nazis were being elected to the town council and soon Bauhaus budgets began to be cut again. Gropius resigned and Ludwig Mies van der Rohe, an architect, succeeded him as head of the school.

Shortly before Hitler became Chancellor, Mies moved the Bauhaus to Berlin and turned it into a private school. He hoped that by avoiding state subsidies he could keep the school out of state politics. But the Nazis continued to attack it as a "hotbed of degenerate, cultural Bolshevism." As the attacks grew more vicious, Mies closed the school. Most of the faculty left Germany. Many, including Gropius, Breuer and Mies himself, came to America where their influence on American architecture and design has been enormous.

Most of the Berlin theatre people and many of the writers liked to think of themselves as left-wing intellectuals. True or not, there is no doubt that most were definitely on the side of democracy and social and economic reform. There were a few lesser literary and theatrical figures who sided with the Right and wanted a return to Bismarckian order, discipline and imperialism. They started out by decrying the weaknesses of democracy, then they began to protest the carnival spirit in Berlin. Finally they wound up echoing Hegel in praise of war as a cleansing process for the soul. Few of them became known beyond their own circles.

One of the few who was read outside of Germany was Oswald Spengler, author of *The Decline of the West,* published in 1926. Spengler believed that world cultures arose, reached their peaks and died, like the seasons, and that one had no connection with its predecessor or its successor. He thought that all of Europe was in its dying stage and had no use for attempts at the revival of Europe through democracy.

Rainer Maria Rilke, Germany's great lyric poet who died the same year *The Decline of the West* appeared, did not like the revolution or the Republic either, but not because he sided with the forces of reaction. He thought Germany could only be reborn through humility and he did not be-

77

lieve republican Germany differed much from Imperial Germany. "She did not acquire that dignity which springs from the deepest humility," he wrote. "She was concerned only with salvation in a superficial, hasty, distrustful and grasping sense. . . . She wanted to persist, and not to alter."

During Hitler's Third Reich, most of the liberal, republican and left-wing writers, theatre and film people fled from Nazi Germany. Fear of persecution or the search for a climate of intellectual and political freedom sent them to countries all over the world, especially the United States. The great rebirth of the arts in Germany had its brief period of glory, then collapsed with the rise of a new authoritarian government.

The 1920's had seen an extraordinary artistic development in Germany. And the period of 1924–1929, the good years, had seen the best of that development. Those were also the good years of the Weimar Republic in general. The economy seemed to be on more solid foundations, and optimism ran high. Gustav Stresemann seemed to be the one man in the country who might succeed at stabilizing the political situation. If the governing political parties could be kept in balance—and if nothing happened to upset this delicate equilibrium—then the affairs of state could be run in an efficient, sensible way.

6 Stresemann and the Politics of Hope

THE GOOD YEARS FOR THE Weimar Republic had really begun in August 1923, when Stresemann became Chancellor, though it was early 1924 before the effects of his policies became noticeable. The new Chancellor had moved with dispatch, first calling off the passive resistance in the Ruhr. When this had been settled, a temporary arrangement was worked out between France and the Ruhr industrialists that allowed reparations payments to be resumed. Both actions were designed to placate the Allies, particularly the French, so that the government could turn its attention to other pressing domestic problems.

Stresemann had taken office at a moment of political turmoil and uncertainty. There had been rioting in the Rhineland, where the French had been encouraging a separatist movement. Communists had joined governments in the states of Saxony and Thuringia, hoping that this would be a springboard to national power. Add to this the events in Bavaria, which would later be climaxed by Hitler's abortive Munich putsch, and the temper of the country seemed violent and unpredictable.

So if Stresemann had any doubts about what he should

The aftermath of a separatist riot in the Rhineland. The separatists, encouraged by the French, wanted to secede from Germany and form their own state.

do to stem this rebellious tide, his doubts were settled when a Communist-led uprising erupted in Hamburg on October 23, 1923. Though it sputtered out in failure, rumors began to swirl about a possible Communist take-over in Saxony. Stresemann acted swiftly. Upon his urging, President Ebert, invoking Article 48, issued a decree dissolving the Saxon cabinet. Army units seized the state's capital and the coalition cabinet of Communists and Social Democrats was deposed. A new one was just as quickly organized, consisting solely of Social Democrats, and the emergency was at an end.

Stresemann's behavior during this crisis made one thing patently clear: he would take decisive action if and when he deemed such action necessary.

Next, the intrepid Chancellor tackled the runaway inflation. Actual stabilization was put into the hands of Minister of Finance Hans Luther and Hjalmar Horace Greeley Schacht, a forty-six-year-old economist who had been active in financial and trade circles since before the war. Schacht, as Special Currency Commissioner, immediately halted the printing of all paper money. He introduced an interim currency, the *Rentenmark*, valued the same as the old pre-war mark. It was covered by mortgaging the entire agricultural and industrial resources of the country. In other words, the German people put up everything they owned as security to back it. Some observers called this a display of patriotism; others dismissed it as a colossal bluff but, regardless of motive, it worked. In fact, the speed with which it worked raised grave questions in many minds as to why the inflation had happened—or been allowed to happen—in the first place. However, that didn't help the vast middle class, whose life savings had long since been spent in the inflation.

Germany was now on a comparatively sound course. The threat of civil war was over and the mark was on the way to dependability. Schacht, who was now thought of as a financial wizard, was made head of the Reichsbank. As for Stresemann, his reward was different. For his boldness and energy, for his part in putting down the Communists and fighting the inflation, he was set upon in the Reichstag by his critics of the Right and Left. Toppled by a vote of no confidence, he resigned as Chancellor but stayed on as Foreign Minister in cabinet after cabinet, and continued to support the Weimar Republic.

Only three months later, his successor, Wilhelm Marx of the Catholic Centre party, felt it was safe to end the state of emergency.

However, the French still occupied the Ruhr; the Germans still couldn't meet the reparations payments, and the new Rentenmark needed more solid backing than mortgaged property.

In April 1924, after three months of study, the Dawes Committee issued its report on Germany's finances and its recommendations for improving them:

First, her money must be sound before she could even try to meet her foreign debts and so the Committee called for a

Hjalmar Horace Greeley Schacht, named after a famous American newspaper editor, won a reputation as a financial wizard in the inflationary twenties. When the Nazis took power, Schacht became Hitler's Finance Minister.

new currency, the *Reichsmark*, which had the same value as the temporary Rentenmark, but was controlled by a Bank of Issue independent of the German government. Then, assuming a stable currency, the Committee figured that Germany should be able to pay out 240 million dollars the first year and more each successive year for four years until the annual payments reached 600 million dollars. This amount could be adjusted up or down after that according to Germany's state of financial well-being. Security for the payments was to come from bonds of state railways and other industrial enterprises, plus revenue from custom duties and taxes on alcohol, sugar and tobacco. In order to stabilize the value of the Reichsmark on the international market, payments were to be made in marks and the Allies, to whom they were paid, would be responsible for changing them into their own currencies.

To make sure everything worked as planned, the Reparations Commission appointed Allied Commissioners to the Bank of Issue and to the management of those industries whose tax payments were earmarked for reparations. The

Commission also specified that an Agent for Reparations Payment be in overall charge.

Last, but far from least, the French were to leave the Ruhr promptly and Germany was to receive a foreign loan of 200 million dollars to do two things—provide a currency reserve and help pay for the first reparations installment, which would be due before the benefits of the plan had begun to take effect.

In March, in the aftermath of Hitler's Beer Hall putsch and Stresemann's resignation, Ebert had dissolved the Reichstag and called for new elections. The primary issue became the Dawes plan.

The right-wing Nationalists campaigned against the plan because it gave foreigners a say in German business affairs. Stresemann campaigned for it, saying that Germany must rid herself of her financial chains and earn the goodwill of the rest of the world. Elections were held in May and the plan's opponents won. The Nationalists picked up thirty more seats in the Reichstag, and the Nazis polled enough votes to be represented in the Reichstag for the first time. (It was in this election that Ludendorff won his seat as a Nazi deputy.) The Communists also increased their strength. The Social Democrats, the People's party and the Democrats all lost seats. Nevertheless, the Reichstag approved the Dawes plan, 247 to 183.

The whole plan was then submitted to an international conference in London and accepted without difficulty. In addition, Stresemann got an agreement from the Allies that they would never again penalize Germany unless she deliberately failed to meet her obligations.

The German loan was issued in October 1924. In France it was taken up privately by banks. Everywhere else it was subscribed to—oversubscribed to, in fact—by private investors, more than half in the United States and more than one-quarter in Great Britain. In mid-November 1924, the French withdrew from the Ruhr. Except for Allied troops

German reparation payments were an urgent issue in 1924. Here, Stresemann's successor as Chancellor, Dr. Wilhelm Marx, is shown attending an international conference in London that discussed the problem.

in the Rhineland, as specified by the Versailles Treaty, and Allied overseers in a handful of German industries, as called for by the Dawes plan, Germany was once more master of her own house.

The Dawes plan had many strong points, which everyone hailed. It limited its demands to sums a prosperous Germany could conceivably pay. It removed reparations from politics by treating them as if they were ordinary commercial debts. It gave the Allies the security of knowing that

84

payment was sure because they knew where the payment money would come from. It insured the maximum amount of impartiality in administering payments by putting it all into the hands of the Agent for Reparations Payment— especially since that agent was an American.

But the plan also had its weak points, which were at first overlooked. One of its errors was to put foreigners in charge of Germany's finances. It also provided for annual payments without specifying how many, when they would end, or what the sum total would be. And it put Germany in the hopeless position of knowing that any increase in her prosperity would mean an increase in her reparations debts. There was thus no incentive for her to save, for any savings would only go to the Allies, sooner or later. But worst of all, it established a precedent for borrowing foreign money to pay foreign debts.

As a result of the Dawes loan, Germany went on a borrowing spree. During the next five years nearly every German city and German industry borrowed heavily, mostly from the United States. Almost eight billion dollars flowed in, while only two billion dollars were being paid out.

Not only did the extra six billion dollars go toward reviving industry, it also financed public works, extended social services, and subsidized agriculture. Cities built huge stadiums, swimming pools, racing fields for bicycles and motorcycles, great new complexes of apartment houses, opera houses and other cultural and recreational facilities.

The government started encouraging scientific research in the universities. Business boomed, money in circulation grew, wages went up and union membership increased. The cartel system, in which manufacturers of similar products got together to fix prices, divide up the markets among themselves, control production, regulate foreign trade and sometimes even pool profits, was enlarged to include foreign competitors. This was designed to cut down competition, stabilize prices, protect investments and avoid boom-and-bust cycles. The most famous of the cartels, the vast chemical enterprise, I.G. Farben, controlled almost 400 firms in Germany and nearly 500 abroad.

Few people had the foresight to recognize that Germany was paying her debts with American money and that her prosperity depended on the continued popularity of German loans in Wall Street, a rather unreliable source of support.

The bulk of the German reparations payments, made out of this American money, went to France and Britain. They, in turn, used the German reparations to pay off their debts to the United States, so the United States was, in effect, paying its debts to itself.

It seemed to Stresemann that achieving German financial health solved only half the problem. The other half, still awaiting solution, was just as important, if not more so. For if Germany could not work out some agreement with her neighbors that would enable her to live at peace with them, then economic recovery and other domestic triumphs would not matter in the long run. The diplomatic front had to be secured before the nation—and the Republic—was really secure.

Stresemann's predecessor as Chancellor, Wilhelm Cuno, had first proposed in late 1922 that Germany sign some sort of regional pact guaranteeing the western border of Germany. This, he had hoped, would give France that sense of security she seemed to need so badly (after all, she had been invaded by Germany twice in two generations). But Cuno didn't pursue the idea. Stresemann did.

He figured that if the Germans recognized—and admitted —that Alsace and Lorraine were again French and would remain so, and also guaranteed the *status quo* along the Rhine, France would be satisfied. She might even cooperate with Germany in solidifying other international relationships. In February 1925, Stresemann sent official notes to

86

France and Britain suggesting such a pact. London was interested. Paris was, too, if Germany would agree to join the League of Nations. This would presume Germany's acceptance of the borders of fellow League members.

Then Stresemann ran into trouble at home. The new Chancellor, Hans Luther, who had succeeded Wilhelm Marx, had taken the Nationalists into the cabinet for the first time because of their success at the polls in the May 1924 elections. The Nationalists were violently opposed to renouncing German claims to Alsace and Lorraine. So was the Army. General von Seeckt stated frankly: "We must acquire power and as soon as we have power, we will naturally retake all that we have lost."

For some time the reactionary elements, who had never accepted Ebert as their president, had been circulating slanders about him. In 1925, Ebert was forced to sue for libel. He had been having attacks of appendicitis but he didn't want to go to the hospital for an operation while his suit was pending. Finally, the suit was tried and Ebert won. By then it was too late for surgery. His appendix had burst and he died of peritonitis, at the age of fifty-four.

Seven men decided to run for his office—among them one former Chancellor, one former cabinet member, one state president, one Communist Reichstag deputy and General Ludendorff. No one received the required majority, so, under the constitution, a run-off election was necessary.

The Nationalists suggested Hindenburg, now retired, as a national figure who stood above party differences. Stresemann did his best to discourage the idea. He knew that to the Allies Hindenburg symbolized the Prussian lust for war, which they had spent four years defeating. He was afraid this would set back his diplomatic efforts. But the Hindenburg supporters were more persuasive. The old man decided to run and Stresemann's People's party eventually, if reluctantly, supported him. The democratic center and left-of-center parties joined forces behind one of the candidates

87

from the first round, ex-Chancellor Wilhelm Marx. The Communists renominated their candidate—which turned out to be a crucial decision.

Four weeks after the first election, Germany voted again. Hindenburg won 48 per cent of the votes, not a majority, but in a run-off only a plurality was required. Had the Communists opposed anti-republicanism in a meaningful way by backing Wilhelm Marx instead of syphoning off left-wing votes for their own nominee who couldn't possibly have won, Marx would have been elected and the history of Germany might have been different. In fact, Marx could have won if only *half* the votes that went to the Communists had gone to him. It was that close.

Hindenburg, though, surprised both his supporters and his critics. He may have hated the idea of a democracy and the government he now headed, but he had taken an oath of office and an oath was sacred to a Prussian.

"I have taken my new important office," he stated in a proclamation after his election. "True to my oath, I shall do everything in my power to serve the well-being of the German people, to protect the constitution and the laws, and to exercise justice for every man. . . . My office and my efforts do not belong to any single class, nor to any stock or confession, nor to any party, but to all the German people . . . ."

For the next five years he showed a most careful respect for both the letter and the spirit of the constitution. The monarchists and militarists were furious but—momentarily —helpless.

In October 1925, Stresemann's negotiations with the British and the French paid off. At Locarno, in Italian-speaking Switzerland, a whole series of treaties were signed providing for the *status quo* (or as Stresemann preferred to call it, "maintenance of peace"). In the first pact—between Germany, France and Belgium—these three countries promised

The new President of the Republic, Paul von Hindenburg, makes his inaugural speech to the Reichstag on May 19, 1925. The former commander of the Kaiser's armies assumed the office at an advanced age after the death of Friedrich Ebert.

not to go to war to alter boundaries. In four additional pacts—with France, Belgium, Poland and Czechoslovakia—Germany agreed not to try to change her eastern boundaries by unilateral action.

The Nationalists promptly resigned from the cabinet in protest but the Reichstag approved the treaties, 300 to 174, anyway. It also approved Germany's application to the League of Nations by a vote of 275 to 183, despite Nationalist and Communist objections. (Though their ultimate objectives were different, the Nationalists and the Communists were beginning to find common ground in their efforts to bring down the Republic.)

Aristide Briand of France and Gustav Stresemann of Germany, two key figures at the Locarno Conference in 1925. For their diplomatic efforts on behalf of a peaceful Europe, they were jointly awarded the Nobel Peace Prize in 1926.

Stresemann, defending his position, said, ". . . a nation must not adopt the attitude of a child that writes a list of its wants on Christmas Eve, which contains everything that child will need for the next fifteen years. The parents would not be in a position to give it all this. In foreign politics I often have the feeling that I am being confronted with such a list, and that it is forgotten that history advances merely step by step, and Nature not by leaps and bounds . . . ."

In addition to the obvious contents of the Locarno treaties, there were some others not only unspoken but, for a while, unrecognized.

There was, for instance, the implication that this second guaranteeing of boundaries, being voluntary, was morally more binding than the original guarantees of the Versailles Treaty. This weakened the value of the Versailles Treaty. Then, because Britain didn't sign the treaties pertaining to Germany's eastern borders, the impression arose that Britain wasn't interested in territorial integrity as such, that she considered some borders more important than others and would only come to the defense of those she cared about. This created a bad precedent and in ten years' time a lot of nations would act as if there were no reason for them to defend a frontier in which they were not personally and immediately concerned.

Overall, the Locarno treaties encouraged the view that the Versailles Treaty needed other agreements, voluntarily arrived at, to make it effective. But at the moment of signing, the merits seemed to outweigh these hidden flaws.

For the first time since 1918, Germany was being recognized as a member of the family of nations. Britain's Foreign Secretary, Austen Chamberlain, described the Locarno agreements as "the dividing line between the years of war and the years of peace." Others agreed with him. In 1926, Germany's Gustav Stresemann and France's Aristide Briand shared the Nobel Prize for Peace. That same year Germany was formally admitted to the League of Nations. Her rehabilitation seemed complete.

The Russians now began to worry that Germany, by joining the League, had negated the Rapallo agreement. They were afraid that if the western powers attacked them, Germany, as a League member, would have to join in. So Stresemann signed another treaty with Russia. It reaffirmed the terms of the Rapallo pact and promised that each country would remain neutral in the event of an attack on the other. This made what had been merely a statement of friendship into an alliance.

The Reichstag endorsed it unanimously. The British approved, thinking it might bring the Russians into closer contact with the League to the benefit of all concerned. But the rest of Europe began to look suspiciously at Germany again. The rest of Europe wondered whether the new agreement might not nullify the provisions of Locarno. The French, probably coincidentally, began to build the Maginot Line, a series of underground fortresses along the French-German frontier, which were supposed to be impregnable.

91

Two days after Germany's formal acceptance into the League of Nations, Stresemann addressed the world body in Geneva. "The most durable foundation of peace," he said, "is a policy inspired by mutual understanding and mutual respect between nation and nation. The German government is . . . glad to see that these ideas, which at first met with lively opposition in Germany, are now becoming more and more deeply rooted in the conscience of the German people. . . ."

The next major international agreement Stresemann signed was the Pact of Paris, sometimes called the Kellogg-Briand Pact after the American Secretary of State Frank Kellogg and French Premier Aristide Briand. It quite simply renounced war as an instrument of policy. The six Great Powers (United States, Great Britain, France, Italy, Germany and Japan), the three other Locarno powers (Belgium, Poland and Czechoslovakia), plus the British Dominions and India, all signed it. Almost every other country in the world, including the Soviet Union, enthusiastically endorsed it. In 1924, Stalin had adopted the slogan, "Socialism in one country." Trotsky, the advocate of world revolution and Stalin's most bitter foe, had been eased from power. With the fires of European rebellion dampened for the moment, Bolshevik strategy underwent a profound change. The Russians now set about putting their own affairs in order at home. Their slogan, in effect, became: Russia first. World revolution was shelved, temporarily, until the historical situation would shift again in favor of the communists. Reflecting this new mood and policy, the USSR signed the Pact of Paris as a gesture of its goodwill.

The only remaining German grievances were the Allied occupation of the Rhineland, due to last till 1935, and that still-festering wound, reparations. As a member in good standing in the League of Nations, Germany pressed harder for a solution, and since she was now on friendlier terms with her former enemies, a solution seemed possible. Even the French agreed that if a final settlement of Germany's financial obligations was negotiated, occupation of the Rhineland could be cut short. So another committee was set up to finish what the Dawes Committee had started.

This delegation, too, was headed by an American lawyer and businessman, Owen D. Young. The Young committee started work in February 1929 and issued its recommendations in June.

The Young plan called for thirty-seven annual payments of 500 million dollars each, somewhat smaller than the amount the Dawes plan called for, to be followed by twenty-two smaller payments to cover what the European Allies owed the United States. Payments would thus continue until

French soldiers inside the Maginot Line, the underground defense system built by France along her common frontier with Germany. This vaunted, supposedly impregnable barrier against German attack failed to halt Hitler's legions in 1940.

1988. The foreign control that the Dawes plan had imposed on Germany would end but the Germans would have to reassume the responsibility for transferring the payments from marks into foreign currencies. And, finally, the Young plan recommended a Bank of International Settlements to be set up in Switzerland to receive and distribute the payments.

In August 1929, the conferees met again in Holland to arrange for an actual end to the occupation of the Rhineland. According to their plan, the final Allied soldier would be withdrawn by June 30, 1930. (Actually the troops were all out by May 17, 1930, but the event was overshadowed by the troubled world situation.)

The Germans were still resentful. They didn't see why they, their children and their children's children should be saddled with reparations payments for another fifty-eight and one-half years, especially since they didn't admit to any "war guilt," despite the Versailles Treaty clause. Schacht repudiated the Young plan, although he had originally signed it, resigned from the Reichsbank in protest and went over openly to the Nazis.

"The German people had the right," he wrote, "to expect the foreign governments to cease their efforts to squeeze out of German industry special payments and sacrifices . . . . We must ask the German government . . . before it finally accepts the Young plan, to balance the budgets of the national government, of the states and of the municipalities and to provide for a reduction in the burden borne by the German people as will make it possible for German industry to live."

Still, the last of the big questions hanging over German heads—reparations, foreign control of their industries, occupation of their territories—had seemingly been answered and, for the first time since the summer of 1914, Germany was a free and sovereign nation at peace with her neighbors.

But this moment of freedom and prosperity did not last long. Within a couple of months Germany was dealt two

94

unrelated blows from which she was never able to recover.

On October 3, 1929, Stresemann, the man of moderation and diplomacy, whose cool head and farsightedness were soon to be needed more than ever, died of a stroke. He was only fifty-one. His years of labor to sustain the Republic that he never really wanted in the first place had killed him. Three weeks later, on October 24, the New York stock market crashed.

For several years the prices of common stocks of American companies had been increasing at a very rapid rate. People of every income level were speculating in them as if the Stock Exchange were the two-dollar window at the local race track. They would buy on margin, putting down as little as 10 per cent of the cost of the stock. Their brokers put up the rest which, in turn, they got from the banks. Thus a man could buy $100,000 worth of stocks for only $10,000, sell it as fast as possible at a higher price and pay the broker back the $90,000. If he had sold at $150,000, he would net $50,000, or a profit of 500 per cent on his original investment.

Business though, despite the optimistic words of the government, wasn't really good enough to warrant the prices at which the securities were selling. The wild speculation drove prices higher and higher until they went so high that the investors didn't—or couldn't—buy anymore. They began to sell. With so many speculators selling there were few who wanted to or were able to buy. Since 90 per cent of the investment money had come from the brokers, they wanted their money back and called for more margin from their customers. If the customers couldn't supply it, the brokers sold their stocks to recoup what they could. Paper profits vanished. Big and little investors alike were wiped out.

Suddenly there was no more American money to invest in German loans to build German industries, improve German cities, buy German goods or pay German debts. The rock on which Germany's prosperity had been built turned out to be made of *papier mâché*.

7 Right, Left and Center

LITTLE BY LITTLE, DURING THE SIX YEARS from 1923 to 1929 —the Stresemann years, as they came to be called—the Germans drifted to one political extreme or the other. The middle-of-the-road parties, except for the Catholic Centre, which had its adherence to the Church to hold it together, steadily lost strength. The depression, resulting from the crash of the American stock market, speeded up this process.

Those who opposed the Republic did so for many reasons. All they had in common was dislike for the existing government. The Republic's supporters consistently underestimated the opposition and never mustered enough strength to counteract it.

Among the opponents were those who disliked democracy to start with: the monarchists and the militarists who wanted a return to the glorious days of Bismarck and the Kaiser; and the Communists who thought Weimar was a "bourgeois creation" in which the workers were still exploited by the capitalists. The Communists believed that the only road to what they called "pure democracy" was through a dictatorship of the proletariat that would gradually become a socialist state either by evolution or revolution, but in either case under their leadership.

Others objected to parliamentary rule, claiming it no longer applied to the twentieth century, though they weren't sure why. Others didn't like the fact that republicanism was a form of government copied from other western countries. They resented and resisted western influence.

Another group wanted what it called "total democracy without liberal principles." This seemed in some twisted way to make democracy and dictatorship compatible.

Still others objected to the rash of political parties in the Weimar Republic. Actually there were only seven major parties, but there were over 100 splinter and regional groups which, even together, never totaled more than 14 per cent of the Reichstag. Spengler spoke scornfully of the Republic as a "business firm" whose laws referred only to parties and not to people. He was wrong, but those who found so many parties confusing, believed him.

It is true that German political parties were hard to keep track of. Periodically, the left wing of one would split off and merge with the right wing of another, or vice versa. Sometimes the names were radically altered. Sometimes the change was just enough to create more confusion. Seldom did the name of a party reflect its platform, and often it meant just the opposite of what the party stood for. For instance, there was a National Liberal party that was really conservative, and a National People's party that wanted to restore the monarchy. There was another People's party that believed in private property first and people second, and the National Socialist German Workers' party that was really fascist.

There was a group that opposed the Republic because it objected to middle-class values such as mass production of goods and making money. These people called their view *Lebensphilosophie* or Life Philosophy. The Life Philosophers, like Luther, were against reason and thinking. They

A synagogue in Berlin is defaced by vandals, part of the Nazi hate campaign against the Jews.

wanted to return to primitive "folk" communities and be led by a "folk leader" who had risen from the people and would be guided by his heart, not by his head. This to them would be true "German" democracy, "non-western" and "non-Jewish."

Germany's Jews numbered only one per cent of the population. Most of them had been German for centuries, but to many of their fellow Germans the Jews were still aliens and foreigners. One has only to remember the racism of Luther and Fichte, the murder of Rathenau by the Bavarian Frei-korps, and the emotional response evoked by Hitler's doctrine of race hatred, and German anti-Semitism stands revealed as a tradition that infected the national blood-stream. Like a virus, it might lie dormant for years, only to flare up again during periods of stress and crisis. A prominent and educated Junker of the time wrote: "There is no doubt that the Weimar Republic and the democratic party suffered serious harm from the fact that the great democratic press was in Jewish hands. This led to an identification of Jewry with democracy, which was bound to be fateful for both of them."

98

What was infinitely more fateful for democracy than the fact that German Jews supported it, was the wiping out of the middle class by the inflation, and then the downward economic spiral that resulted from the abrupt ending of American investments and loans.

Overnight, foreign customers for German goods disappeared, with the single exception of Russia. Communist Russia's entire economic life was regulated by the government and was less affected by the economic troubles elsewhere. In fact, this apparent stability during the worldwide depression was one reason why so many people were favorably disposed toward Communism in the desperate days of the 1930's.

With the disappearance of foreign money, Germany could no longer finance her industrial expansion or pay her foreign debts. With the disappearance of foreign customers for her goods, there was no money to buy from abroad the food and raw materials she needed to feed her people and her factories. The factories produced fewer goods and needed fewer people to produce them. Businesses went bankrupt. Banks failed. More people were laid off. Fewer people had money to spend. So the roller coaster continued downhill: fewer sales, smaller profits, smaller staffs, still more unemployment, unpaid bills, and one million teenagers, who would soon be voters, coming out of school with no hope of anything but going on relief.

Skilled workers who had survived the inflation couldn't survive this latest crisis. Even the labor movement, the backbone of the Republic, was now divided into The Employed and The Unemployed.

Labor union members had the cushion of some unemployment insurance payments, which kept them going for a while. But the small shopkeepers, who were going bankrupt, the professional people, and the intellectuals had no place to turn and nothing to look forward to. The one thing they had clung to in the past to keep up their morale and maintain their self-esteem was the fact that the laboring classes were worse off than they. Now that was no longer true and it was more than they could take.

Hungry men wandered the streets, wondering how they could feed their families. Some committed minor crimes so they could be arrested and sent to jail where they would get a hot meal. Others joined Hitler's *Sturmabteilung*—the infamous Storm Troops—for food and the free uniforms.

In September 1929 nearly 2,000,000 people were out of work. One year later there were 3,500,000. In 1931 the figure rose to nearly 5,000,000 and in 1932 to more than 6,000,000. That was more than the combined total of unemployed in all Europe. When Germany went to the polls in 1932 to elect a president for the third time, nearly half its adult male population was jobless.

The country was in despair, but Hitler's mood was one of elation. "Never have I been so well disposed and inwardly contented as in these days," he wrote in the Nazi party newspaper.

The ex-corporal had come a long way from the early days of political struggle. Just a few years before, as he languished in prison for his part in the Beer Hall Putsch of 1923, the outlook had seemed dark indeed. Others had carried on in his place, most notably his second-in-command, Gregor Strasser. With the official party banned, Strasser and a few other key Nazis had formed the National Socialist German Freedom Movement as a cover for their continuing political activities.

Strasser was a Bavarian by birth, a druggist by profession, and a war hero. During the war he had risen from the ranks to Lieutenant and had won an Iron Cross. In 1920 he joined the Nazis, attracted by the socialist parts of their program. Much to Hitler's distress, he took this aspect of the Nazi creed seriously. He didn't take seriously, though, Hitler's claim to personal dictatorship, and he refused to defer to him, which distressed the Nazi leader even more.

100

But Strasser was an invaluable aide and Hitler needed him. Eventually, however, he came to distrust and finally dislike his number-two man.

Strasser had a jovial manner and liked good living. He was also a born organizer and an effective public speaker. He wanted to build the party around the common man and he didn't see why the Nazis shouldn't team up with anyone, even the Communists, if their interests coincided. Hitler found these ideas shocking. Yet, in the last days of the Republic, the Nazis did just that.

The National Socialist German Freedom Movement ran candidates in the May 1924 elections, taking a stand against the Dawes plan. It won enough votes locally to become the second largest party in Bavaria. Nationally, it polled 2,000,000 votes, enough to give it representation in the Reichstag for the first time. One of the 32 seats it won went to Strasser. That was before Stresemann had stopped the inflation. Once the inflation was curbed and life became easier, the Nazis' new-found strength began to ebb.

Two weeks before Hitler came out of jail in December

Hitler's number-two man, Gregor Strasser, did not always agree with the Leader. He was later murdered in the bloody purge of 1934.

1924, there was another election. This time the Nazis won only 1,000,000 votes, a drop of 50 per cent in six months. It was obvious that they needed disasters on which to feed.

Hitler, promising to be law-abiding, persuaded the Prime Minister of Bavaria to lift the ban on the party. "The wild beast is checked," said the Prime Minister. "We can afford to loosen the chain." But at the first party gathering after that, the "wild beast" showed no signs of being checked. His speeches against the Republic were so violent that the Bavarian government promptly, forbade the Nazi leader to speak in public for two years. So Hitler concentrated on organizing the Nazi party, readying it to seize the government when the time came.

First he went after dues-paying members. By the end of 1925 he had 27,000; by the end of 1929, and the beginning of his final surge to power, he had 178,000. He also courted the big industrialists, the men with money and right-wing political views.

In a series of private meetings arranged by Hermann Goering, one of his lieutenants with aristocratic connections, Hitler convinced big industry, some of them members of Alfred Hugenberg's Nationalists, that he had their interests at heart, and that the "socialist" in his party's name didn't really mean anything.

Hugenberg's Nationalists were already Nazi in sentiment. Except for the fact that they were largely aristocratic—Junkers, Army officers and high-ranking civil servants—they would have been outright allies. But the Nationalists were also snobs and looked down on the Nazi "rabble," although they found it expedient to work with them to destroy their common enemy, the Republic.

Then Hitler built a party structure to correspond to the structure of the government itself. For administrative purposes he divided Germany into districts paralleling her election districts. He also set up a couple of extra districts for other countries with sizeable German minorities, on

102

which he already had his eye. He divided each of these districts into circles, the circles into local groups, the local groups into street cells and blocks. Politically, he set up departments to correspond to the various agencies of the government—agriculture, justice, labor, foreign affairs, press, and other key ministries.

The Nazis, who tended to be rowdy and vulgar among themselves, objected to bringing women and children into the party, so Hitler organized special groups for them, as well as groups for students, teachers, civil servants, lawyers, doctors and artists. He also organized a second armed force, more reliable than the unruly S.A. who were constantly feuding among themselves. This was the *Schutzstaffel,* or S.S., whose members took an oath of loyalty to Hitler personally, rather than to party or country.

In 1927 Hitler was permitted to speak in public again and promptly began a new round of campaigning and troublemaking. But in the election of May 1928, with Germany prospering and on good terms with her former enemies, the Nazis got a mere 800,000 votes, worth 12 seats in the Reichstag, fewer than half of what they had received four years earlier.

Brown-shirted Storm Troopers made up the goon squads of the Nazi movement. Training sessions, such as this, taught them all the skills of brutality, terror and violence.

The Communists also welcomed the results of the Wall Street crash. They thought it would speed up the coming of their revolution.

The German Communist party had followed some tortuous turns in word and deed since its founding on December 30, 1918. At its initial meeting the first split in its ranks developed. The left-wing extremist branch of the party, whose overriding aim was an immediate and successful social revolution, disregarded the advice of the party founders and leaders, Karl Liebknecht and Rosa Luxemburg. The extremists voted not to participate in the elections for the assembly, which was to draw up the constitution.

After the murders of Luxemburg and Liebknecht two weeks later, this revolutionary wing continued to set policy for a few months. They were singularly unsuccessful. Not one of the positions they took won any public support. The only reason the party didn't collapse and disappear altogether was that social conditions in Germany were so chaotic. The demoralized people kept looking for new answers and some thought that Communism might be one solution. So the party kept attracting new members.

Then the moderate wing, which wanted to cooperate with other working-class parties, especially the Social Democrats, and work for economic and social reform rather than revolution, took over the leadership for a while. This drove out the most extreme Communists, who formed their own splinter group, the Communist Workers' party. The leader of the moderate wing eventually left the party, too, and rejoined the Social Democrats.

The rest of the Communists, still under moderate leadership, then joined with the left wing of the Independent Socialists, a considerably larger and more important group. The combined elements adopted a new name: the Communist Party of Germany. For the first time there were enough of them—nearly 400,000—to be considered a mass movement.

104

Communist party boss Ernst Thaelmann, wearing Red Front uniform, gives clenched fist salute as he marches with his followers. Communist policy during the twenties kept shifting from threats of militant action to periods of moderation.

The party went through several more switches in policy from moderate to revolutionary to moderate and back again, until in 1925 it became completely subservient to Russia's Communist party. From then on its changes in policy and tactics were dictated by Stalin. In those years Stalin was fighting Trotsky and his advocacy of "world revolution." After Trotsky's defeat, the German Communists prudently stopped advocating his policies.

In 1929, when Stresemann died and the depression struck,

the party line changed again. Stalin now predicted the collapse of capitalism. The Communists fully expected the people to flock to them. They turned out to be fatally wrong. In the words of an old German saying, they had "added up their dinner check without asking the innkeeper," the innkeeper in this case being the people. More people went over to the Nazis than to the Communists, and the trade unionists, who should have been the backbone of any mass people's movement, stayed loyal Social Democrats.

The Reichstag, in the meanwhile, had been trying to cope with the country's growing economic woes but was not doing a very good job of it. Small though unemployment insurance was, the conservatives wanted it cut. They blamed the country's financial troubles on too much spending for the social welfare program. The Social Democrats, who once again had the thankless task of steering the country through a time of disaster, refused. But even they had their doubts. They knew the budget should be balanced, but they also knew they couldn't let down their working-class supporters.

The Reichstag haggled over the unemployment insurance question well into 1930. It also haggled over the Young plan. Without Stresemann's calming influence the arguments grew more bitter. Finally, on March 27, 1930, after the Reichstag finally accepted the Young plan, Chancellor Hermann Mueller resigned. Since the Social Democrats were obviously unable to get enough support to govern, President Hindenburg picked Heinrich Bruening, the parliamentary leader of the Catholic Centre, to succeed Mueller.

The Catholic Centre was still primarily concerned with the well-being of the Catholic Church. It had both industrialist and trade union members and, with such conflicting interests under one roof, it kept vacillating, forming coalitions with parties on the Left or on the Right depending on the issues in question. It supported private property and opposed socialism. Yet it voted for health and unemployment insurance. It could never decide how much democracy it really wanted, how earnestly it should support the Republic, and which of its basic positions should be—or could be—compromised for the sake of a coalition. In the end, it was willing to compromise quite a few.

As the Nazis gained in strength, the Catholic Centre advocated a "popular assembly" in which all parties, including the Nazis, should be represented, on the widely held, but mistaken theory that the Nazis could be "controlled" or "tamed" by being given responsibility. The party leaders even conducted talks with the Nazis to try to figure out what they really wanted and whether a coalition was possible.

Bruening's selection as Chancellor had been engineered by the Army. A hitherto unknown "desk" officer, a protégé of General Groener named Lieutenant General Kurt von Schleicher (whose name in German means "intriguer") had recommended Bruening to the aging Hindenburg. Schleicher was a personal friend of Hindenburg's son, Oskar, and one of a group who thought the only way to save Germany was to make the President as powerful as the Kaiser had been. Schleicher claimed to speak for the Army, which, for the most part, had done its politicking behind the scenes. He was to have a brief moment in the political limelight.

Bruening, an economist, was a deeply religious man and a war hero. After the war he had a hard time deciding whether to go into politics or into the Church. He chose politics and joined the Catholic Centre party. By 1929, as the depression struck, he was its parliamentary leader.

Bruening was sober and conservative, qualities that the Army heartily approved. Due to his economist's training, he relied on logic and statistics as political weapons; his opponents, however, employed traditional political means, using eloquence and backstage deals, with more success. Bruening's cabinet, which leaned decidedly to the right, contained no Social Democrats, the first time this powerful party had not had such representation since the inception of the Republic.

Sober, conservative Heinrich Bruening, parliamentary leader of the Catholic Centre Party, became Chancellor in 1930. His cabinet—which contained no Social Democrats—had a decided rightist slant.

Bruening presented to the Reichstag the deflationary program the Social Democrats had rejected—lowered unemployment insurance, reduced pensions, price and wage controls, and other measures that could balance the budget. When he couldn't get Social Democratic support, he wooed the Nationalists. A popular joke of the time was: "Why is Bruening

108

President Hindenburg's order dissolving the Reichstag is read to its members. This day, July 18, 1930, marked the beginning of the end of parliamentary government in Germany.

like a guitar?" "Because he is held by the left hand and played by the right."

To get the Nationalist support he recommended a program called *Osthilfe* (help for the East), to make government loans to the large but impoverished landowners in East Prussia. This appealed to Hindenburg, who had recently

109

acquired a huge tract of land there. On his eightieth birthday he had been presented with the estate in the East that had been the ancestral home of the Hindenburgs.

Despite conservative support, Bruening still couldn't get his program passed. Few deputies wanted to go on record in favor of something that was sure to be so widely unpopular. But Bruening was convinced that his way was the only road to salvation. In June 1930, he asked President Hindenburg to declare a state of emergency under Article 48 and then sign the program into law by presidential decree. On July 15 Hindenburg did as Bruening requested. The Reichstag promptly demanded that the presidential decree be withdrawn, one of its constitutional privileges. On July 18 Hindenburg dissolved the Reichstag and called for new elections.

That date marked the close of a chapter in postwar Germany's political life. Although voters would continue to go to the polls and cast their ballots in a long series of elections, parliamentary democracy had entered its twilight phase. It would come to a sudden end on March 5, 1933, when the nation held its last free election.

PART III
The Final Years (1929-1933)

8 Rise of the Radicals

THE SEPTEMBER 1930 ELECTION CAMPAIGN WAS hectic and noisy. When the votes were counted, the Nazis had done far better than Hitler had expected. He had hoped to win 36 more seats for a total of 48. Instead, the Nazis won a staggering 95 more for a total of 107. They were now the second largest party in the country. The Communists jumped in strength, too, but not nearly as much. They moved to fourth place with 77 seats.

The Social Democrats, still the largest party with 143 seats, had suffered a decline of 10 seats. The newly formed State party, a merger of the Democratic party, which Rathenau had founded, and the liberal wing of the People's party, which Stresemann had founded, had hoped to attract all moderates into one strong political movement to support the government. It sought to be a true consensus party instead of a spokesman for special interests. But the voters didn't want a consensus. They preferred special-interest spokesmen and gave the State party only 20 seats, five fewer than its predecessor, the Democratic party, had won in 1928.

Private political armies were growing, too. In addition to the Nazi S.A. and S.S., there were the *Stalheim* (steel hel-

Many political parties had private armies. The Stalheim (Steel Helmets), shown marching here in Berlin, were the military units of Alfred Hugenberg's Nationalists.

mets), a veterans' group organized by the Nationalists, the *Red Front Fighter's League* of the Communist party, and the Social Democrats' *Reichsbanner* Black-Red-Gold, which the rank-and-file had organized in despair over their leaders' inaction in the face of the right-wing danger. These armies kept in trim by fighting each other. One of the Nazi slogans, in wide use during the "final years," was "Possession of the streets is the key to power." The battles of the streets far outnumbered the battles of the ballot boxes, and in the end they were more decisive.

The police did little to stop the brawling, except to intercede occasionally and perhaps reduce the actual number of fights. To really restore order would have required strong measures, and strength was one thing the federal government did not have. The larger states of Prussia and Bavaria were beginning to complain about the federal government's failure to prevent disorders. They threatened to take steps within their own areas of jurisdiction if the government didn't.

During the winter of 1930-31 everything grew worse—the economic situation, the people's morale and the public disorder. There was little Bruening could do to improve the financial state of the country or the lot of its citizens. He also failed to keep the various political factions happy. He couldn't reach any kind of a compromise with the Nazis because their idea of compromise was to do it their way, and Bruening, despite his lack of imagination and flexibility, was basically opposed to everything the Nazis stood for.

He made one attempt to ease the economic situation by proposing a customs union with Austria. The tariffs of the two countries would be coordinated and, together, they would be better able to fight the depression. Politically, they were to remain completely separate. The rest of Europe screamed in protest, fearing that the two countries would not remain politically separate for long if they linked their economies. For more than a century, the Allied powers had been opposed to just such a colossus dominating Europe. Eventually, the question was referred to the World Court at the Hague, which vetoed the proposal by a vote of eight to seven. Meantime, as if to prove how valuable such a customs union could have been, Austria's principal bank failed and the German banks that had investments in Austria began to teeter.

As a result, America finally realized that it was unreasonable to expect impoverished Germany to continue to pay punitive war debts. Herbert Hoover, who had arranged the feeding of the hungry in Europe and Russia after the war, had been sworn in as President of the United States just six months before the stock market crashed. He now persuaded the Allies, even the reluctant French who still nursed their hatred of Germany, to suspend reparations for a year.

Both the Nazis and Communists were profiting by the

people's misery. State elections in 1931 brought more successes to the Nazis. They became the second largest party in Saxony. They now held key positions in the police force in Thuringia, and they won control in Brunswick. Brunswick promptly granted German citizenship to Hitler, something he had never bothered to do for himself in all these years. With a presidential election coming up in 1932, he was now eligible to run.

The Communists, too, were winning more votes, although their gains were nowhere near as great as the Nazis'. They were never the actual threat the Nazis made them out to be.

In October 1931, all the parties of the Right gathered in the little Brunswick town of Harzburg. Their purpose was to form a united front to get rid of Bruening. Nationalists, spokesmen for heavy industry, Junkers, representatives of the *Stalheim,* some princes and other nobles, and of course the Nazis, were there. Hitler gained some respectability by being included in this socially acceptable company. His contribution, in return, was the support of the Nazi masses.

Meanwhile, Bruening, who knew his government was the most unpopular Germany had had since 1919 (he was called the "Hunger Chancellor" because he had cut unemployment insurance and pension benefits), tried to find a way out that would improve morale and bring prosperity and stability back to Germany.

He thought of trying to negotiate a cancellation of reparations after Hoover's moratorium year was up. He thought of trying to persuade the Allies at a disarmament conference scheduled for 1932 in Geneva to either honor the Versailles Treaty by disarming to Germany's level or to allow Germany to rearm up to theirs.

He also considered restoring the monarchy. Bruening knew that if Hindenburg, already eighty-four and failing in health, were re-elected, he could not be expected to survive another seven-year term. Should he die in office, Hitler could still run in the interim election and might win. So

114

Bruening proposed that they call off the 1932 election and extend Hindenburg's term, which could be done by a two-thirds vote of the Reichstag. Then the President could proclaim a monarchy with himself as regent. Upon his death, one of the sons of the Crown Prince would come back as a constitutional monarch. This was designed to take the wind out of the Nazi sails. Bruening even got reluctant support from the Social Democrats for such a plan. But Hindenburg would have none of it.

Still loyal to the Kaiser, he wouldn't even consider a restoration of the monarchy, unless it was the Kaiser or the Crown Prince who were restored. Bruening pointed out

The forces of the Radical Right meet to organize a united front against the forces of the Radical Left. The gathering of Hitlerites, Nationalists and Junker elements, which took place in October 1931, in the mountain town of Bad Harzburg, was celebrated afterward by this parade of Nazi troops.

that the democratic segments of German society would never accept either of them. Hindenburg ordered him from the room.

General Schleicher, still intriguing behind the scenes, thought the time was now right to introduce Hitler to Hindenburg. Hindenburg found the Nazi leader an "unmannerly upstart." Bruening offered Hitler a cabinet post if he would promise not to run against Hindenburg for President. Hitler refused. For him, it was to be all or nothing. He was sure that before long it would be "all."

The end result was that at eighty-five, and not at all eager for the strains of a political campaign, Hindenburg had to run again, to save the Republic. One wonders if he appreciated the irony of the situation—that he was now saving the Republic from the radical Right instead of the radical Left?

Much to his distress, monarchist, militarist, Junker, Protestant Hindenburg found himself supported by the Social Democrats, the Catholic Centre, the trade unions and the remnants of liberal, democratic, middle-of-the-road parties. The Nationalists, the monarchists, the Junkers, even the former Crown Prince himself—with whom Hindenburg's sympathies really lay—were against him.

There were two more unexpected candidates, neither of whom had the slightest expectation of winning. They hoped to take just enough votes away from the two principal contenders to prevent either from winning a majority, thus forcing a second election. One was the Communist party leader, Ernst Thaelmann, and the other was Colonel Theodor Duesterberg, the second-in-command of the Nationalists' Stalheim.

The Communist party line, which came from Moscow, charged that the Social Democrats, by upholding existing law and order, were moving farther and farther to the right. The Communists began to lump them together with the militarists, monarchists and reactionaries in what they termed a Fascist United Front. The Communists were fully

116

The race for the presidency in 1932 pitted Hindenburg against Hitler. Posters like this appeared all over the country.

convinced that their only path to power lay in bringing down the Weimar Republic. The Social Democrats, staunchest supporters of the Republic, were the chief obstacle. So they, instead of the Nazis, became the Communists' primary target. The Communists were perfectly willing to cooperate with the Nazis to defeat and destroy their common enemy.

The race for the presidency set a new pattern in political campaigning for Germany. Earlier in the year, Hitler had addressed the Industry Club, whose membership included all the steel and coal barons. He spoke for two and a half hours, denouncing democracy, defending private property, warning against the "Red Menace," and promising to lead Germany back to "faith and ideals." As a result, the Nazi coffers were now overflowing with contributions from heavy industry. The Nazis were able to distribute 8,000,000 pamphlets and 12,000,000 extra copies of their party newspapers.

117

They staged 3,000 meetings a day all over the country and, for the first time in German electioneering, used films and sound trucks.

Bruening worked equally hard for Hindenburg. He abandoned his usual sense of fair play and reserved all the time on the government-controlled radio networks for his own side. The Nazis were furious. Hitler was unable to make a single national broadcast. Hindenburg spoke only once, the night before the election, but most effectively. He said, "Election of a party man representing one-sided extreme views, who would consequently have the majority of the people against him, would expose the Fatherland to serious disturbances. . . . Duty commanded me to prevent this. . . ."

Hindenburg won 49.6 per cent of the vote, fractions short of the absolute majority he needed. Hitler got only 30.1 per cent. Thaelmann received 13.2 per cent and Colonel Duesterberg, 6.8 per cent. The minority candidates had accomplished their objectives. Now there would have to be

Apartment dwellers in the Communist section of Berlin called on citizens to vote for their party's candidates on election list number "4".

WIDE WORLD

another election and this time Hitler might win.

The Nazis had increased their vote by 5,000,000 over the 1930 election, but it still wasn't enough. Party propagandist Goebbels thought they were through. But Hitler, in the next day's party newspaper, announced jubilantly, "The first election campaign is over. The second has begun. I shall lead it."

For this second campaign he introduced another "first." He chartered an airplane and flew from one end of Germany to the other, giving rise to the slogan, "Hitler Over Germany." He addressed three or four big rallies a day in as many cities. He altered his message to attract more voters. Before, he had harped on the misery of the people and the inability of the Republic to do anything about it. Now he painted rosy pictures of the future—more jobs, higher prices for farmers, a big Army, more business for the businessman. He even went so far as to promise every German girl a husband.

This time the Nationalists threw all their support to Hitler instead of running their own candidate. The Communists, though, ran their own man again, as they had in 1925. On April 10, 1932, Hindenburg won the election again with a handy 53 per cent of the votes cast. Hitler's vote rose to 36.8 per cent, a bigger percentage increase than Hindenburg's but he wasn't even close. The Communist candidate lost support. He polled only 10.2 per cent.

From the statistics it looked as if the people had spoken decisively. They had rejected both extremes. Hitler had scored astonishing successes—he had doubled the Nazi vote in two years—yet, in the depths of depression and at the height of civil unrest, he couldn't win a majority. Some in his party, especially the moderate Gregor Strasser, argued that the best course for the future lay in making a deal with the victors, that Hitler would never gain power through a democratic election.

Except for the hard-core Nazis, the rest of the country

119

A meeting of Nazi leaders after the election loss to Hindenburg in 1932. Gregor Strasser, sitting on Hitler's left, wanted the party to make a deal with the victors, but Hitler refused.

agreed with Strasser, and everyone, from the center to the left, and even some to the right of center, breathed deep sighs of relief.

In addition to disagreeing with Strasser's view of the political situation, Hitler had developed a deep distrust and dislike of the man who had once been his chief lieutenant. Hitler didn't like Strasser's socialist ideas; he was jealous of Strasser's achievements as a party organizer and of his triumphs at the polls, and he resented the affection and esteem he commanded among party members generally. Strasser, for his part, was getting more and more disillusioned as Hitler grew more and more dictatorial.

While the Nazis were confidently preparing for their expected victory, the authorities had been studying various documents that had been coming into their possession. These documents indicated that the Nazi Storm Troopers

120

were preparing a putsch that would be followed by a reign of terror. This secret plan was scheduled to go into operation the day after the election—if Hitler won.

On Election Day, as the people were streaming to the polls to cast their votes for moderation, Hindenburg's Minister of War, General Groener, who had come back into the government in 1928, outlawed both the S.A. and S.S. The German states, which had been asking for just such a crack down, were pleased. Schleicher had first approved it, too, but once the deed was done he abruptly shifted his position. He really wanted to incorporate the Nazi private armies into the Reichswehr where he could control them. He also wanted Hitler in the cabinet where he thought he could control him, too. Schleicher told Hindenburg that Groener's act had been a mistake. A coolness then developed between the President and Groener.

Some of the Nazis wanted to rise in rebellion at once, but Hitler shrewdly persuaded them to wait. He was counting on Schleicher to "intrigue" Groener and Bruening out of office.

The Nazi leader did not have long to wait. His unwitting accomplice was Hindenburg. Instead of saving the Republic, the aged President now began to dig its grave. One month after the election, he disposed of General Groener, and two weeks later Bruening was dismissed.

Groener had been the target of a smear campaign, both whispered and in the press, ever since he banned the S.A. and S.S. On May 10, 1932, he rose in the Reichstag to defend his action. Goering leaped to his feet to lead the attack on the General and the rest of the Nazi deputies joined in. Groener was already a sick man. The viciousness of the Nazi opposition made him sick at heart as well. On his way out of the building Groener bumped into Schleicher, who told him the Army no longer had confidence in him and that he should resign.

Thirteen years before, Groener had taken the responsibility of telling the Kaiser he must abdicate, thus sparing Hindenburg the unpleasant duty that should have been his. As a result, Hindenburg remained a national hero, his reputation untarnished. Now Groener appealed to his former commander for the support he thought he had earned. The President expressed his regret but said he could do nothing. On May 13, bitter and disillusioned in both his old chief, Hindenburg, and his old protégé, Schleicher, Groener resigned.

Now it was Bruening's turn. For a month, the intriguers had been laying the groundwork. Hindenburg's son, Oskar, told his father that Bruening's new land reform program would take land from some of the bankrupt East Prussian Junkers and open it up for settlement by the landless and hungry peasants. Schleicher told him the country really needed a more flexible Chancellor who could control the Nazis. The industrialists complained about Bruening's economic policies. Hindenburg listened. On May 29, he dismissed his faithful Chancellor, of whom he had said not so long before that he was "the best since Bismarck." Goebbels wrote in his diary that everything was proceeding according to plan.

From then on events moved at breakneck speed. There was probably more intrigue during the last nine months of the Weimar Republic than had occurred in its first thirteen years.

9 The Triumph of Adolf Hitler

BRUENING'S SUCCESSOR AS CHANCELLOR WAS Franz von Papen, also a Schleicher nominee. Papen was witty, charming, rich and aristocratic. Through his wife he knew many important people in industrial circles. During World War I he had been military attaché in Washington until President Wilson demanded his recall for illegal and conspiratorial activities. Among other things, Papen had tried to blow up some American munitions plants.

Papen was a member of the conservative wing of the Catholic Centre. He disapproved of his party's collaboration with socialists and liberals. The party came to disapprove of him and ultimately expelled him. He was socially popular but not even his best friends gave him high marks as a politician or a diplomat. That didn't bother Schleicher, who really wasn't looking for a man of ability. He wanted a puppet. He had been singing Papen's praises to Hindenburg, Hugenberg and Hitler for some time.

Papen packed his cabinet with his aristocratic friends, including Schleicher, who came out from behind the scenes to be Minister of Defense. The cabinet read so much like a *Who's Who in German Nobility* that it was promptly nick-

123

Franz von Papen, who succeeded Bruening as Chancellor, was helped to power by General Schleicher.

named the "Cabinet of Barons." It had a few industrialists and militarists, too, mostly members of Hugenberg's Nationalists, but not a single representative of the working class.

On June 4, 1932, five days after he had appointed Papen, Hindenburg dissolved the Reichstag again. His reason was that it no longer represented the national will and he felt that another election should be held. Papen himself issued a proclamation, in which he stated that his government was trying to form a front of all patriotic elements in the country. He said the country had been ruined by the Versailles Treaty, the "mismanagement of parliamentary democracy," and the increase in state socialism, which produced "moral disintegration of the people, aggravated by class warfare and cultural Bolshevism." This kind of language sounded suspiciously Nazi in tone and content.

Next, Hindenburg lifted the ban on Hitler's private armies, as Schleicher had quietly promised the Nazis he would. They fought the Social Democrats' *Reichsbanner.* The Nazis started most of the brawls, protesting all the while that they were innocent victims. They charged that the Communists were being led by members of the Russian secret police. They demanded a "free hand" to protect themselves. They said the local police had lost control and insisted that the S.A. be given permission to "clear the streets." Germany was close to civil war.

The climax came on July 17, 1932, in one of the poorer working-class districts in a Hamburg suburb, where the Communist party had a sizeable membership. The Nazis decided to march in uniform through the area, knowing perfectly well that it would infuriate the Communists and immediately took to the streets again and the number of street fights and political murders mounted all over the country during the election campaign. Most of the clashes were between Nazis and Communists, but the Nazis also

Storm Troopers carry a sign reading "Death to Marxism." Demonstrations like this one often ended in street brawls between Nazis and their leftist opponents.

provoke violence. As Hitler's troops came into sight the Communists in the area opened fire from rooftops, windows and balconies. The Nazis and their police escort fired back. Several of the combatants were killed, many more were wounded. The government blamed it all on the Communists.

These riots gave Papen an excuse to do something he had been wanting to do for some time—bring Prussia, Germany's largest state with the best-trained police force in the country, under federal control. This would be a severe blow to the Social Democrats, for Prussia was their last political stronghold.

The Prussian question had been in the news for several months. The last local election in April had been a Nazi triumph. They had won 162 seats. The Social Democrats had taken only 94. The Nazis demanded the premiership but they didn't have a majority. They needed the Catholic Centre's 67 votes. The Centre said it would cooperate with any group that would abide by the constitution, but it would fight any attempts to impose a dictatorship. Since the Nazis admittedly intended the latter, no compromise was possible. The defeated Social Democratic government therefore stayed on in office until the impasse could be broken. In June, Papen ordered Prussia to pick a premier at once, knowing perfectly well that Prussia could not comply while its parties continued to disagree.

After the riots, Papen summoned the acting members of the Prussian cabinet and told them they weren't enforcing law and order. Under emergency powers given him by the President, he removed the Social Democratic premier and his Minister of the Interior and appointed himself Federal Commissioner for Prussia. The Minister of the Interior hotly denied Papen's trumped-up charges and refused to give up his job. The federal government then declared martial law in Berlin, which was the capital of Prussia as well as of the Republic. It gave the local divisional commander of the Reichswehr what amounted to dictatorial

126

powers. Chancellor Papen was confirmed as Commissioner for Prussia and authorized to remove all the Prussian ministers from their offices. The government decree explained why such extreme action had been necessary. The recent disorders, it said, were due to Communist agitation and Prussia wasn't sufficiently anti-Communist.

The whole maneuver was clearly unconstitutional and the Social Democrats were again faced with an emergency decision. After the Kapp putsch in 1920 the trade unions had struck and saved the government. Would the same tactic work again? The Communists were in favor of such a strike but the Social Democrats refused to go along. Relations between the two parties had reached the point where they would not cooperate even on minor matters. The fatal quality of this split, and its fateful consequences for the country, was now starkly revealed. Indecision also played its role. The combat battalions of the Social Democrats, the Reichsbanner, were ready to take to the streets and fight the Nazis to the death. These armed units had been organized for just such an emergency. But the party leaders held back, fearful that they might provoke a civil war. In the end no one did anything.

German Social Democracy, since the birth of its party in 1875, had always been imbued with humanitarian, democratic principles and a strong faith in reason. It was, in addition, strongly pacifist in its sentiments and instinctively shied away from violence. Its leaders now decided that reliance on the voting booths in the upcoming July 1932 election would be a wiser way to defeat the Nazis than a resort to arms. But by their failure to act—and that meant open warfare in this case—they had conceded the field to Hitler. Their lame explanation was that they did not wish to give Papen an excuse for calling off the elections. The Nazis had no such fears, nor were they concerned about democratic niceties. They had no intention of abiding by the verdict of the electorate if the vote went against them. So, in choosing peace

127

instead of war, the Social Democrats threw away their last chance to save the Republic.

Meanwhile, an international economic conference had opened at Lausanne, Switzerland. Final settlement of the reparations question was one of the key items on the agenda. What Bruening had hoped to prove was now obvious to everyone except France, namely that Germany could no longer meet her payments. The conferees persuaded France to agree that reparations demands should be dropped forever if Germany paid three billion gold marks into a general fund for European reconstruction. Reparations thus came to an end, fifty-four years ahead of schedule.

The election campaign went into high gear around mid-July. Hitler took to the skies again, flying from place to place, addressing more than three mass meetings a day.

Members of the Reichsbanner hold a mass meeting outside the Reich-stag building. These combat sections of the Social Democrats called for armed conflict against the Nazis but their party leaders wouldn't let them fight.

These rallies were professionally staged. Second-string Nazis would whip the crowds to high emotional peaks. Then there would be the distant hum of an airplane, and presently Hitler himself would emerge from the darkened entrance to the meeting, arm held out stiffly in front of him in the Nazi salute, and walk slowly down the center aisle toward the platform in the beam of a single searchlight.

On election day the Communists gained enormously at the expense of the Social Democrats, who were now paying for their indecisive behavior in Prussia. The Social Democrats fell back to second place among the parties. The Catholic Centre made slight gains, the only comfort left to those who supported the Republic. The State party, only two years old, almost disappeared. It won four seats. The Nationalists were down to 37 and the People's party to seven. These last 44 votes were all that Papen and his mentor, Schleicher, could count on.

The Nazis made the greatest gains to become the country's largest party, with 230 seats, but they still didn't have a majority. More than half of the German people still didn't want them. Their total, in fact, wasn't much more than Hitler had won in the presidential race three and one-half months earlier. Despite their increase in Reichstag seats, the Nazis seemed to be standing still. Those who had been saying that Hitler had already reached his peak were congratulating themselves on their judgment.

Now that his government had been soundly beaten, Papen stated that he wouldn't mind including a Nazi or two in his cabinet. The Nazis demanded the Chancellorship and the principal ministries. Hindenburg refused. (In addition to personally disliking Hitler, he had been told by the Foreign Office that other countries were becoming alarmed about developments in Germany and that some of them might take "drastic action" if Hitler were named Chancellor.) Papen then offered Hitler the Vice-Chancellor's post. Hitler rejected it.

In the summer election of 1932, Hitler conducted an intensive campaign. This time he was determined to win.

Knowing that the divided Reichstag wouldn't be able to function, Papan got a document from Hindenburg authorizing him to dissolve it at his discretion. It was the first time a Reichstag was ready for dissolution before it had even assembled.

The Reichstag met on August 30, 1932, and elected Hitler's right-hand man, Goering, as Speaker. Then it adjourned for two weeks. When it met again, the Communists, always willing to cooperate with the Nazis when it suited them, presented a motion of no-confidence in Papen. Goering, equally willing to join hands with his sworn enemies, called for an immediate vote. Papen demanded to be heard but

Goering ignored him. Papen then placed the decree dissolving the Reichstag on the table in front of the Speaker. Goering refused to look at it. He took the vote and the government lost overwhelmingly, 512 for the no-confidence motion, 42 against. Goering then pronounced the dissolution decree meaningless since the government had already fallen. Papen, with Hindenburg's backing, took the reverse position. The *vote* was meaningless, he said, because the Reichstag was already dissolved. He ordered new elections to be held in November.

Parliamentary procedures in Germany were becoming a tragic farce.

The people were tiring of these constant campaigns and elections. So were the party workers who had to do the campaigning. The only one who seemed to enjoy them was Hitler.

Hitler, as usual, outshouted all the other campaigners. Hugenberg's Nationalists, who had been less generous lately with their financial contributions, were now added to his list of targets and roundly attacked. Papen was the culprit who had persuaded his Nationalist friends to stop giving money to Hitler until the Nazi leader abandoned his all-or-nothing position.

Papen's election tactic was to emphasize the non-party character of his government. The Communists tried, with considerable success, to win converts from among the extremist Nazis who resented Hitler's failure to seize the government by force. They also recruited Social Democrats who had been disillusioned by their party's lack of action.

On November 3, three days before the election, the transport workers in Berlin went out on strike to protest a threatened wage cut. The Social Democrats disapproved but the Communists backed the workers. So, to everyone's astonishment, did the Nazis. The Nazis announced piously that they could not allow the living standards of the German workers to fall below those of "Chinese coolies." Nazis and

*Franz von Papen shown at a Steel Helmet meeting with other National-
ist leaders. It was he who convinced his friends in these rightist circles to
stop their financial support of Hitler.*

Communists stood side by side on street corners shaking little
boxes in which they collected pennies for the strikers. The
Nazis, as a result, lost not only considerable middle-class
support but also a lot of contributions from anti-labor busi-
nessmen.

The election results demonstrated that the German people
still didn't want Hitler. The Nazis polled 2,000,000 fewer
votes than they had three months before and lost 34 of their
seats. The Nationalists, the only ones to support Papen,
picked up nearly 1,000,000 more votes, obviously from the
Nazis, for a total of 52 seats. The Communists climbed to
100 seats. The Social Democrats lost 12 seats. They now
represented a mere 20 per cent of the Reichstag. Only the
Catholic Centre held its own.

All those who had worried about the phenomenal growth
of the Nazis now became concerned about the gains scored
by the Communists, although Communist increases couldn't
compare in size or speed to the recent surge of the Nazis.
The Nazis were the most worried of all. They were running
out of money. They were running out of recruits. They were
losing local elections and they were losing members.

Papen was full of self-confidence, which didn't please
Schleicher. Schleicher still wanted a National Front, with

132

Hitler included He disapproved of Papen's strategy of continually dissolving the Reichstag and calling for new elections until the opposition was worn away. He thought the inevitable result would be civil war. The Nazis didn't want any more elections, either. They were afraid of still more losses. Strasser tried again to convince Hitler that he should stop competing for votes and settle for a deal with those in power.

Schleicher persuaded the rest of the cabinet to join him in demanding Papen's resignation. He had more difficulty with Hindenburg, who had taken a great fancy to Papen. Schleicher, who kept in secret touch with Strasser, relayed to the gullible old President alarming stories about the Nazi trend to revolution and the drift of dissatisfied Nazis toward the Communist party. He told Hindenburg that Hitler was having trouble controlling his impatient followers and that only personal differences between Papen and Hitler stood in the way of a National Front.

Cabinet pressure finally compelled Papen to resign. Papen was sure no one else could form a government. He confidently expected to be recalled, which would make him much stronger than he was now.

Hindenburg and Hitler conferred once more. Again Hitler demanded the Chancellorship and full power. And again Hindenburg refused. He said his conscience wouldn't allow him to give so much authority to the leader of a party that was so hostile to him and his program. Hindenburg's conversations with other party leaders were equally unsatisfactory. He was ready to recall Papen, as Papen had expected. Then Schleicher stepped in.

Another Papen government, he said, would mean another dissolution of the Reichstag and another election, or else an attempt to govern unconstitutionally. Public opinion might turn against the government in either case and there could well be a civil war. He produced an Army survey that said the Reichswehr could not maintain transporta-

133

The Papen cabinet photographed here after it had resigned. General Schleicher, the man in uniform, intrigued behind the scenes to force Papen's ouster.

tion and supplies if there were a general strike. Nor could it guarantee law and order if there were a civil war. He suggested that some other Chancellor might be able to work out a National Front government. Several other cabinet ministers backed up Schleicher by refusing to serve under Papen. Hindenburg finally gave in. Schleicher now began to search around for another puppet Chancellor he could control but Hindenburg prevented this. If Schleicher were so opposed to Papen, he suggested, then he had better take on the job himself.

Schleicher became Chancellor on December 3, 1932. Immediately, his troubles began. He had no organized following. No party or faction, nationally or locally, supported him. The President was cold and disapproving because he had scuttled the presidential favorite, Papen. And the Reichstag was bound to be difficult.

Schleicher, the intriguer, now had to intrigue for himself. He opened up talks with the major parties and political factions in the country, including the Nazis, hoping to put together some kind of coalition. He offered Strasser the post

134

of Vice-Chancellor, hoping thereby to entice the support of the Nazi moderates. By this maneuver, Schleicher sought to cause a split in the National Socialist ranks between the Strasser faction and Hitler's more extreme followers. Strasser, scenting an opportunity, was eager to accept Schleicher's offer. But Hitler would not allow it.

Angrily, he accused Strasser of treason. Strasser denied it. The two Nazis exchanged hot words. Then Strasser went home to write Hitler a long letter in which he unburdened himself of everything he had forgotten to say during their quarrel. He relinquished his party positions and resigned from the party itself. He also gave an interview to the local newspaper explaining why he had resigned, so the Nazis couldn't even keep his defection a secret. Then he left for Italy. The Nazis were terrified. They were afraid he might well split the movement.*

Unable to form a coalition with the Right, Schleicher turned to the Left. He approached the trade unions, offering all kinds of concessions on wages, prices and farm assistance. But by this time no one believed him. The Junkers were especially furious because he had threatened to publish a damaging report on *Osthilfe,* Bruening's scandal-ridden aid program for the impoverished East Prussian landowners. There had apparently been vast misappropriations of funds.

At this point, Franz von Papen came back into the picture. His mission in life had become Schleicher's downfall. Taking advantage of the favorable political climate, he channelled industrialist and Junker hatred of the new Chancellor into a revived Harzburg Front.

Papen arranged a meeting with Hitler on January 4, 1933, at the home of a Cologne banker. A group of coal and steel barons, headed by steel magnate Fritz Thyssen, agreed to pay Hitler's debts. Papen did not promise Hitler the Chancellorship in a new government. All he wanted at

*One of Hitler's first acts after he consolidated his power in 1934 was to have Strasser arrested and killed in his jail cell.

that moment was to find out what kind of a cabinet Hitler would support. Hitler, with all his recent failures in mind, agreed to anyone as Chancellor so long as he could approve the Minister of Defense.

Schleicher learned about this secret meeting just as Strasser was returning from his brief visit to Italy. Ex-Nazi Strasser agreed to join a Schleicher cabinet. Hugenberg did, too. For a moment the wily Schleicher thought he had succeeded in forming a government. But the Catholic Centre refused to join any cabinet that included Hugenberg. Then the Nazis won a local election and Hitler immediately became less cooperative and more demanding.

The Reichstag was due to meet again on January 31. Schleicher, still without majority support, asked Hindenburg to dissolve it again, conveniently forgetting that one of the arguments he had used against Papen was the danger of taking such a step. But Hindenburg remembered. He refused Schleicher's request. Schleicher knew he was defeated. He resigned on January 28, one day before he had planned to make public the findings of the *Osthilfe* investigation. (The report was never released.)

Schleicher's final word was to urge that Hindenburg appoint Hitler as Chancellor.* Since Papen had organized the Cologne meeting behind his back, he was more opposed than ever to his former protégé.

The Catholic Centre agreed to accept a Hitler cabinet if it conformed to parliamentary principles. Papen agreed to let Hitler be Chancellor with some strings attached. There would only be three Nazis in the cabinet, although the Ministry of War would go to a Nazi sympathizer. Papen would be Vice-Chancellor and sit in at every conference between Hitler and Hindenburg. The leader of the Stalheim would be in charge of the Labor Ministry and

*Hitler would reward Schleicher for his part in bringing the Nazis to power by having him slain in the same blood purge of June 1934 in which Strasser was murdered.

The Nazis triumph. After Hitler had been chosen Chancellor, a giant torchlight parade celebrated the victory.

Hugenberg would head Economics and Agriculture, which had been fused into a single ministry. Hitler would thus be surrounded by old-line conservatives who, in theory, would keep him governing in a strictly parliamentary fashion.

Hindenburg accepted this arrangement. On January 30, he received Hitler and Papen. Papen told him that Hitler had managed to form a National Front government and the President administered the oath of office there and then. Hitler, until that day a loser, put his hand in Hindenburg's and promised to uphold the constitution.

The Nazis celebrated their unearned triumph that night with a gigantic torch-light parade through Berlin, and Berliners went to sleep with the lyrics of the Nazi anthem, the Horst Wessel song, ringing in their ears:

"The trumpet blows its shrill and final blast
Prepared for war and battle here we stand
Soon Hitler's banners will wave unchecked at last
The end of German slavery in our land!"

137

10 Death of a Democracy

AMERICA ALSO WENT TO THE polls in November 1932 to make an equally fateful choice. She, too, had suffered through three years of deepening depression and mounting despair.

President Hoover had inherited the makings of the depression but the responsibility for steering the country through its days of disaster became his. He seemed as helpless as Bruening. Hoover insisted that the only "moral" way out of the crisis was through self-help. He promised that "prosperity was just around the corner," that soon there would be a "chicken in every pot" and "two cars in every garage." But none of these confident predictions showed the slightest signs of coming true.

Unemployment climbed. It tripled from 4,000,000 in 1930 to more than 12,000,000 in 1932. Businesses kept failing and unpaid rent, food and mortgage payments mounted. Men sold apples on street corners just to earn a few pennies; or they stood in line at soup kitchens for a hot meal that would keep them going as they made the rounds looking for nonexistent jobs. The homeless sought shelter in squalid shacks and lean-tos on empty lots and under bridges, settle-

138

The depression in America produced wasteland communities made up of squalid shacks and lean-tos. These bleak-looking settlements were called "Hoovervilles."

ments that they bitterly called "Hoovervilles." Most business-men felt no responsibility to the general welfare. At the same time they objected to the government assuming any. One prominent auto manufacturer, for instance, maintained that unemployment insurance would merely assure unemployment.

By 1932 only 25 per cent of the unemployed were getting any kind of relief and that was mostly in the form of food handouts. About 2,000,000 homeless people were wandering around the country looking for some kind of work. Hopelessness was a way of life in America, too, and most people held Hoover responsible.

In the spring of 1932, Congress had before it a bill proposing to pay war veterans an immediate war bonus. Such a bonus had been promised for a later date—in 1945—but some congressmen thought it made more economic sense to pay it now, when it was needed. About 15,000 veterans, some with wives and children, travelled from all over the country to Washington to lobby for the bill. They camped on the outskirts of the city and waited. When the bill was defeated.

some 5,000 of the ex-soldiers gave up and went home. The rest stayed on. Congress offered to pay their fares home but most of them had no homes to go back to.

Hoover chose to ignore them. There was some talk that their presence was part of a Communist plot. Finally, there was an accidental scuffle between the veterans and the police, and Hoover could ignore them no longer. He ordered Army Chief General Douglas MacArthur to get rid of them.

The General massed four troops of cavalry, four companies of infantry, a mounted machine-gun squadron and six tanks. He marched them to the camping area. Using tear gas, the troops drove the veterans from their temporary shelters, and then burned down the camp. Three people died, including an eleven-week-old baby, more than 1,000 were gassed, and about two dozen were injured.

The veterans, the wanderers, the unemployed, the hungry, the dispossessed, the desperate, all created a potential for violence. This sullen, angry mood simmered just below the surface of American life in the summer of 1932 as the presidential nominating conventions met.

The Republicans complacently re-nominated Hoover. The Democrats nominated Franklin Delano Roosevelt, Governor of New York State. Roosevelt, an unsuccessful candidate for Vice President in 1920, had also served as Assistant Secretary of the Navy during the war.

As Governor, Roosevelt had established a good record on welfare and conservation but a lot of people thought he was weak. He talked of a "new deal." He said flatly that business *had* to assume the responsibility that went with power and where it failed to do so, government must step in to protect the public interest. "Every man has the right to live," he said, "and this means that he also has the right to make a comfortable living. He may . . . decline to exercise that right; but it may not be denied him."

Two days after the Germans had again rejected Hitler, 57 per cent of voting Americans chose Roosevelt over

140

Hoover. But Inauguration Day was not until March 4, 1933. So the country had to wait four months until the new President officially took office.

In Germany, as we have seen, during this same period, Hitler was pulled back from defeat and handed power by a cabal of intriguing politicians. The new Chancellor immediately called a cabinet meeting. He had a serious problem. Even with the support of the Nationalists he lacked majority control of the Reichstag. He could seek out that majority by coming to an agreement with the Catholic Centre, or, failing that, he could dissolve the Reichstag. This would result in still another election, the fifth in a year for the crisis-ridden nation.

Hugenberg suggested outlawing the Communists, which would reduce the total Reichstag vote by 100. Then the Nazis and Nationalists *would* have a majority. But Hitler didn't want to go that far so soon. When the talks with the Centre proved fruitless, an election became a necessity. Now

Governor Franklin D. Roosevelt at an election rally in New York's old Metropolitan Opera House, before he won the U.S. presidency in 1932.

WIDE WORLD

that he was in a more powerful position, however, Hitler was sure he couldn't lose.

The campaign was intense, violent, dramatic and noisy. The Nazis sponsored mass rallies and torch-light parades. Hitler now controlled the state radio, so he and his lieutenants were able to address the entire nation at their will.

Their propaganda combined lavish promises and fierce attacks against political opponents, Jews and Bolsheviks. The people, thundered the Nazis, had given the bungling Republic fourteen years to prove itself and the results of that experiment were tragically visible. Just give the National Socialists four years in office, they promised, and all problems would be solved. Unemployment would disappear. The hated Versailles Treaty would be ended. And Germany would become a great power again. But to accomplish this, of course, firm measures were necessary. Democracy would have to be suspended temporarily. Afterwards, the electorate was assured, there would be a return to constitutional government.

Hitler also warned of an impending Bolshevik revolution that had to be smashed before it started. (This was a real fear on Hitler's part; he actually believed that such an uprising would take place.) But he still made no move to outlaw the Communists. Their meetings were banned and their newspapers shut down, but the party itself was still allowed to function legally. As for the Communists, they cautiously refrained from any action that might bring the power and the wrath of the state down upon them. They knew, or sensed, that Hitler was trying to push them into an armed rebellion so that he would have a legal excuse to crush them for good.

To provoke the Communists even more—and all left-wing elements as well—the Nazis began to remove republican government officials from posts all over the country and replace them with Nazis, usually members of the S.A. and S.S. They instructed the police to go easy on members of the

A Nazi raid on Communist party headquarters produces arrests . . .

. . . and the capture of various weapons.

143

Nazi private armies and the Stalheim but to show no mercy to anyone on the Left. They also ordered the police to use their guns and threatened to punish them if they didn't. During the campaign at least fifty-one anti-Nazis were murdered. Still, the Communists held back from open acts of revolt.

Then, just one week before Election Day, the Nazis finally got what they wanted. The Reichstag building in Berlin went up in flames. Inside the burning building police found a feeble-minded Dutch vagrant named Marinus van der Lubbe. Van der Lubbe had been picked up once before for arson. Fortunately for the Nazis, he also had Communist connections. The dull-witted van der Lubbe was immediately arrested and tried. The trial dragged on for seven months. In the end, he was convicted and executed.

Hitler claimed the fire was the signal for the long-awaited Communist uprising. How it actually started no one will ever know since everyone who had had any information about it was killed during the next few months. But there is enough evidence to suggest that the S.A. itself set it.

There was an underground passage to the gutted building from the Reichstag President's Palace in which Goering lived. This passage carried the central heating system. Apparently, on the night of February 27, a small detachment of S.A. troops went through this passage to the Reichstag building, where they scattered gasoline and self-igniting chemicals. Then they fled back the way they had come. At the same time, the half-witted van der Lubbe seemed to have found his way into the building and set some small fires of his own. He was probably encouraged to do so by the Nazis, who knew of his previous arrest and his passion for fires. At his trial, where he was convicted and sentenced to death, the defense demonstrated that van der Lubbe didn't have the materials to set such a big fire and, in addition, that the building actually burst into flames within a few minutes after he got there.

144

The memorable night of February 27, 1933 when the Reichstag building burned down. Hitler claimed that the Communists set fire to it, but others suspect it was really the Nazis.

Less than twenty-four hours after the blaze, Hitler had Hindenburg sign an emergency decree "For the Protection of the People and the State." It suspended the sections of the constitution that guaranteed civil and individual liberties. It also authorized the federal government to take over complete power in the states if Hitler decided it was neces-

145

sary, and it imposed the death penalty for a whole series of crimes, including disturbances of the peace by armed persons.

During the last week of the campaign, Bruening spoke up forcefully but no one listened. He announced that the Catholic Centre would resist any overthrow of the constitution. He demanded an investigation of the Reichstag fire, which he regarded as highly suspicious, and he implored President Hindenburg "to protect the oppressed against their oppressors."

On March 5, 1933, the Germans participated in their last democratic election until after the Second World War. And despite terror and intimidation, despite Nazi control of the air waves, they again rejected Hitler.

The Nazis improved their position by 5,500,000 votes but it still won them only 44 per cent of the total. The Catholic Centre, in the face of Nazi persecution during the campaign, increased its votes by about 300,000. The Social Democrats held onto their position as the second largest party, losing only a handful of votes. The Communists lost 1,000,000 supporters, and the Nationalists, led by Papen and Hugenberg, both cabinet members, managed to retain their 52 seats. Together, the Nazis and the Nationalists controlled 52 per cent of the votes, enough for the day-to-day business of the Reichstag, but not enough for what Hitler had in mind.

The day before, on March 5, 1933, the 32nd President of the United States was sworn in. He brought a message of hope.

"Let me assert my firm belief," said Franklin Delano Roosevelt in his Inaugural Address, "that the only thing we have to fear is fear itself. . . . The Nation asks for action, and action now. . . ." If Congress didn't act fast enough, he went on, "I shall ask . . . for the one remaining instrument to meet the crisis—broad Executive power to wage

146

a war against the emergency, as great as the power that would be given to me if we were in fact invaded by a foreign foe."

The entire nation was heartened by these vigorous words. Some government officials left over from the Hoover administration, and some editorial writers, too, were afraid that Roosevelt was threatening a dictatorship. But America had 150 years of democracy behind her, a period during which she had weathered many other grave crises. The Executive powers that Congress granted the new President it gave temporarily, and in time it took them back.

In his first one hundred days in office, Roosevelt and Congress did act fast. Congress passed at least twenty different bills aimed at reviving every phase of the American economy, providing work for the jobless, and balancing the budget. Some of these measures, because of the haste with which they were drawn and passed, proved to be unconstitutional, and in due course the Supreme Court nullified them. Both Congress and the President accepted the Court's decision.

In Germany, however, Hitler had no intention of being a temporary dictator. He planned a dictatorship that would last a thousand years. First, he proposed an Enabling Act that would give his cabinet exclusive legislative powers for four years. This would also give him enough time to dispose of all political opposition. Then there would be no one left to challenge him when he didn't relinquish those powers.

Since this legislation required a constitutional change, it had to be approved by two-thirds of the Reichstag. The Nazis and Nationalists didn't have that many votes. They still needed the Catholic Centre. Hitler could have simply arrested enough opposition deputies, under the emergency decree that Hindenburg had signed the day after the Reichstag fire, to reduce the opposition below the one-third level. But he preferred, for the moment, to stick to the fiction of legality. He persuaded the Catholic Centre to cast its 92 votes for the change. The Centre agreed ("for the sake of

147

The death of a democracy, March 1933. With Hermann Goering in the president's chair, the Nazis take over the Reichstag and the German Republic comes to an end.

the party and the future," as one Centrist put it) on the promise of fair treatment for Catholics, a number of constitutional guarantees concerning education and the courts, and Catholic participation in a return to parliamentary government. The Nazis promptly repudiated these promises.

The vote was 441 for the Enabling Act and 84, all Social Democrats, against. The Reichstag thus turned all its functions over to Hitler. Although the President presumably still had veto power, he had long since passed the point where he could exercise it freely. Democracy in Germany, actually dead for some time, was officially buried on March 23, 1933.

On August 2, 1934, Hindenburg died. He was eighty-seven. Hitler promptly combined the offices of President and Chancellor and became, in name as well as in fact, the sole ruler of the Third Reich.

From that day until April 30, 1945, the day he shot himself in an underground bunker in Berlin, Adolf Hitler was the supreme autocrat of the German nation. No one in German history—not even Frederick the Great and the two Kaisers—wielded such power as this ex-corporal with the Chaplin mustache. If the statesmen of Europe had ever wondered what he would do after he took power, they did not have to wait long to find out. His policy was revenge, his weapon was violence.

First, he subdued his personal and political enemies at home. Other parties were banned and their leaders arrested and often murdered. Then Hitler began to arm. "Guns instead of butter" became the slogan of the Nazi war machine. And when the armies of the new Reich began to march across Europe, they brought more death and desolation to the continent than it had ever suffered in its history.

This, then, was the tragic outcome of the ill-fated Weimar experiment. Democracy had been tried in Germany—and it had failed. But it was not alone in this failure. Elsewhere in Europe, during this same period, there had been similar ventures in free government that had foundered and then died.

The war of 1914–1918 had brought down the royal houses of Europe with a crash heard round the world. From the ruins of monarchy and empire there had arisen a whole new constellation of nations and governments. Many of them had been artificially created by the peace-makers at Versailles. New countries were put together from a welter of peoples, tongues and territories, thus adding to the difficulties of the struggling young states.

Yugoslavia, at best a make-shift country carved out of the Habsburg and Ottoman Empires, was made up of Slavs, Croats, Slovenes and Montenegrins, plus Magyar, German, Albanian and Moslem minorities. In addition to all the different languages, there were two official scripts. Those who could read one usually couldn't read the other.

149

Visitors from one city frequently could not even make out the street signs in another city. The different national groups were constantly quarreling. Finally, in 1929, after a ten-year try at democracy, King Alexander declared that parliamentary government had broken down and set himself up as dictator.

Yugoslavia's neighbor, Austria, now vastly reduced in size, didn't really want independence in the first place. Her real goal was the return of King Charles I, the last ruling Hapsburg, or, failing that, a union of some sort with Germany. But the rest of Europe opposed either move. In 1927 the Republic was shaken by an outbreak of street fighting between its Left and Right extremists. In 1933, Chancellor Engelbert Dollfuss, a conservative with Army backing, finished it off by establishing a dictatorship, which he termed a "Christian state" opposed to a "Red democracy."

Hungary, the other part of the Habsburg Empire, was also a fraction of her former size. She, too, sought a return to monarchy and never gave up hoping for a restoration of the throne. The government even appointed former Admiral Miklós Horthy as regent for the King, even though no king sat on the throne. Her old ruling class survived because all those who had opposed the monarchy were now citizens of the other countries that had been created out of former Hungarian territories. (All those countries, incidentally, lived in constant fear that Charles I *would* return and threaten their independence.) So though the peacemakers intended Hungary to be a democracy, it soon reverted to a semi-fascist state run by the landed gentry and segments of the old nobility.

Then there was Poland. This ancient land had disappeared from the map as a country in the late 1700s when it was divided among the Russians, Prussians and Austrians. The new Poland was reborn with a strong historical hatred for all her former rulers. A battlefield during the war, she

150

had been badly mauled in the fighting between Russians and Germans, and now required vast economic assistance. The paramount problem in this country of entrenched privilege in land was rural reform. But reform was slow in coming. The democratic process bogged down in squabbles and stalemates. And adding to its woes was the high birthrate that aggravated an already grave unemployment problem. In 1926 Josef Pilsudski, Poland's national hero and its provisional President from 1918 to 1921, became impatient with the slow progress of democracy. He came out of retirement and staged a *coup d'etat*. From then on it was he who chose the government ministers. In the different cabinets he formed, he was either Prime Minister or Minister of War. But his title was secondary when it came to the realities of power. No matter what his title, Pilsudski was the iron man of the government who really ran Poland.

The Baltic states of Latvia, Lithuania and Estonia, along with Finland, had been part of the old Romanov Empire. They got off to a bad start. The Bolsheviks from the new Soviet Union and the Freikorps from the new Germany battled each other on Baltic territory on behalf of Baltic right-wing and left-wing factions. In Finland, Baron Carl Gustav Emil von Mannerheim, a national hero and future President, drove out both the Russians and the Germans. Other native Baltic leaders, with some help from the Allies, finally did the same in their countries.

Since none of the Baltic countries were plagued with large aristocracies, and all had had experience with farming cooperatives, their democracies worked quite well at first. Lithuania's was the first to fall. Weakened politically by a feud with Poland and Germany, she abandoned democracy for dictatorship in 1926. Latvia and Estonia held out until 1934, when the economic strain of the world depression and the impact of Hitler's triumph in Germany proved too much.

Only Finland and Czechoslovakia survived among the postwar democracies.

Finland was used to governing herself. As an autonomous province under the Czar, she had been greatly influenced by her Scandinavian neighbors, whose constitutional governments had existed for more than a century. Her democratic traditions were therefore strong enough for her to survive the trouble-ridden twenties, the depression-blighted thirties, the Second World War and even today's Cold War.

Czechoslovakia was but one of the countries formed from the shattered remains of the old Habsburg Empire. She had been one of the most industrialized, prosperous and literate areas of that complex imperial arrangement. As a member of the Austrian parliament said as far back as 1861: "We Czechs have always been a people of individual liberty from the oldest times to the present. . . . We know it best that our nationality and liberty are inseparable." Czechoslovakia's well-trained, experienced civil service kept the country's affairs running smoothly—even during frequent explosions of agitation and unrest by her various minority groups. And perhaps most importantly, she had Thomas Masaryk, her

A huge bonfire blazes in Berlin's Opera Square on May 10, 1933, as the Nazis "burn the books." This is how the new German police state struck at the minds and thoughts of those whose ideas it feared and hated.

greatest freedom fighter under the Habsburgs. Masaryk, a noted historian and statesman, founded the country in 1918 and remained its President until he retired in 1935. Czech democracy lasted until 1939, when it was strangled by the invading Nazis.

The death of democracy in Germany, therefore, was not unique. It had been born, it had struggled, and it had perished like so many other new republics of that period. But the manner of its death was different and so was the totalitarian regime created by the Nazis. Hitler's Third Reich, the police state that he erected on the corpse of Weimar, was like nothing ever seen before on this planet. Yet Hitler's plans and intentions—plain for anyone to see— had been clearly outlined in *Mein Kampf,* the book he wrote in jail in 1924.

There have been other despotisms in the past that sought to control the thinking and behavior of their peoples. They succeeded in varying degrees, depending on existing historical conditions and the extent to which rulers were able to impose their creeds on their populations. But the modern totalitarian state is as different from these older forms of tyranny as today's rocket ship differs from the plane the Wright brothers flew at Kitty Hawk. Modern totalitarianism —best exemplified in the thirties by Hitler's Germany, Mussolini's Italy and Stalin's Russia—seeks to exercise *total* control, so that not even a single crevice is left in society where the human personality can take refuge and function freely. This was the kind of state that Hitler envisioned when he wrote *Mein Kampf,* and it was the model he followed when he built, piece-by-piece, the structure of a Third Reich he thought would last a thousand years.

But even modern totalitarian governments differ in certain important respects. The aspect of Hitler's Germany that set it aside from all others was its primitive racial doctrines, whose main target was the Jews. It was this persecution of a helpless minority, so virulent in its hatred, so appalling in its barbarism, that placed Nazism in a special category beyond the comprehension of other nations and peoples. Never before in history had such intense prejudice been codified into laws that deprived individuals of their rights as citizens, their livelihoods, their homes and possessions, and finally their lives, solely because they were Jewish. Even the dreaded Spanish Inquisition, many centuries earlier, had been more humane, for it, at least, gave a Jew an opportunity to save himself from condemnation by becoming a Christian. But under Hitler and the Nazis there was no way out. Six million Jews were killed in gas chambers that were constructed especially for this purpose. The names of these death camps —where human beings were slaughtered like cattle—will live forever as dark symbols of man's inhumanity to man: Dachau, Auschwitz, Bergen-Belsen, Treblinka, and many others.

Nazi excesses, however, were not confined to the territorial limits of the Third Reich. A driving ambition—central to Hitler's foreign policy—pushed them outward, beyond their own borders. "Today Germany, tomorrow the World," chanted Hitler's youth brigades. A whole generation grew up believing that German destiny demanded the conquest of others, for only in this way could all the Germanic peoples be brought together and the races of Europe purified. So they first claimed, and then seized by force, those lands in which German-speaking minorities lived. Non-Germans in these conquered territories had to bow to their new Nazi overlords. Many were sent off to concentration camps; others were assigned labor tasks that reduced them to little more than slaves. Europe soon learned, in these pre-World War Two years, what it was like to live under the Nazi heel.

Then Hitler made a fatal miscalculation. A series of unopposed victories had fed his delusion that he could move at will across the face of Europe. When he invaded Poland in 1939 he did not expect that England and France would stand against him. But they did and all Europe plunged again into the agony of war. Six years had passed since Hitler's ascension to power. Six more would pass before his German legions, beaten on all fronts, retreated to make their last stand amid the rubble and ruins of Berlin. And there, deep beneath the streets of the city, as the final battle raged, the dead bodies of Hitler and his mistress, Eva Braun, would be burned on a funeral pyre, as he had ordered before his death. Born in violence, the Third Reich died in violence.

The Second World War left much of Europe destroyed. This time Germany did not escape physical damage as she had in the first world conflict. And this time there was no

An elderly Jew caught in the dragnet of a Nazi raid in Berlin. The greatest crime in history—the murder of six million Jews—began with arrests like this in 1933.

doubt about the nature of the German defeat and who had caused it. The European experience with Nazism was over —but at a terrible cost to all who had fought to crush it. Defeated Germany was occupied by the victorious Allies, whose forces stayed for four years before departing.

Today there are two Germanies, the German Federal Republic or democratic West Germany, and the German Democratic Republic or communist East Germany, both established in 1949 when the occupying victors withdrew.

West Germany is still a functioning democracy but in recent years right-wing parties have emerged and an occasional former Nazi party member turns up in a high government position. Only twenty years after the Nazi debacle some of these right-wing groups link themselves openly with the legacy of Hitler and his distorted philosophy. Others trace their political conservatism back further than Hitler— to the Kaiser and the German attitudes that helped the Nazis to rise during the Weimar Republic.

The passions and hatreds stirred up by World War Two have still not died away. Suspicions of German intentions persist, and an atmosphere of caution and distrust continues to surround the relations between the western democracies and the troubled nation that has been called "the key to Europe." As for divided Germany itself—what her future will be, and whether her two halves will ever come together again, cannot yet be predicted.

Bibliography:
A Supplementary Reading List

CARR, E. H., *German-Soviet Relations Between Two World Wars, 1919–1939*, Baltimore, The Johns Hopkins Press, 1951. Also available in Harper Torchbooks paperback.

CARR, E. H., *International Relations Between Two World Wars, 1919–1939*, New York, St. Martin's Press. Reissued 1947. Also available in Harper Torchbooks paperback.

DEHIO, LUDWIG, *Germany and World Politics in the Twentieth Century*, New York, Alfred A. Knopf, 1959. Also available in W. W. Norton paperback.

GRUNBERGER, RICHARD, *Germany, 1918–1945*, London, B. T. Batsford, Ltd., 1964. Also available in Harper Colophon paperback.

HALPERIN, S. WILLIAM, *Germany Tried Democracy*, New York, Thomas Y. Crowell & Company, 1946. Also available in W. W. Norton paperback.

KOCHAN, LIONEL, *Russia and the Weimar Republic*, Cambridge, England, Bowes & Bowes, 1954.

KOCHAN, LIONEL, *The Struggle for Germany, 1914–1945*, Edinburgh, Scotland, Edinburgh University Press, 1963. Also available in Harper Torchbooks paperback.

The Paths of Dictatorship 1918–1933, Ten Essays by German

157

Scholars, F. Stern, ed., Garden City, New York, Doubleday & Company, Inc., 1966.

SHIRER, WILLIAM L., *The Rise and Fall of the Third Reich,* New York, Simon and Schuster, Inc., 1959. Also available in Fawcett Crest paperback.

SNYDER, LOUIS L., *The Weimar Republic,* Princeton, New Jersey, D. Van Nostrand Company, Inc., 1966.

TAYLOR, A. J. P., *The Course of German History,* New York, G. P. Putnam's Sons, Capricorn Giant paperback, 1946.

WISKEMANN, ELIZABETH, *Europe of the Dictators 1919–1945,* London, William Collins Sons, 1966. Also available in Harper Torchbooks paperback.

SUPPLEMENTARY FICTION:

COLES, MANNING, *Toast to Tomorrow*
FALLADA, HANS, *Little Man, What Now?*
HUGHES, RICHARD, *The Fox in the Attic*
ISHERWOOD, CHRISTOPHER, *Berlin Stories*
REMARQUE, ERICH MARIA, *The Road Back*
REMARQUE, ERICH MARIA, *Three Comrades*

158

Index

159

161

A Note About the Author

For more than ten years, *Barbara Sapinsley* has been on the staff of CBS News. Her television credits are many, including several scripts for the well-received "Twentieth Century" TV series and writing assignments for NBC, CBS and ABC-TV. Miss Sapinsley has had her articles appear in such magazines as *Seventeen, Cosmopolitan, Holiday* and *The New York Times Magazine*. Her avid interest in people and places has taken her on many lengthy trips to Europe, the Middle East and the Caribbean.